Contents

Section 1: Introduction

1.0 Changes to this edition of the Guide

The 2018 amendments to this guide introduce revised standards for when gas-fired and oil-fired boilers are installed or replaced in existing dwellings.

These changes affect Section 2 and Section 3 of this document, and parts of this introductory section. No other changes have been made.

1.1 Scope

This guide provides detailed guidance for the installation of fixed building services in new and existing dwellings to help compliance with the energy efficiency requirements of the Building Regulations.

This edition covers the design, installation and commissioning of:

- conventional means of providing primary and secondary space heating, domestic hot water, mechanical ventilation, comfort cooling and internal and external lighting

- low carbon generation of heat by heat pumps, solar thermal panels, and micro-combined heat and power systems.

The guide sets out recommended minimum energy efficiency standards for components of building services systems, including the use of controls. For systems installed in new dwellings, the standards are design limits (or backstop values). For new or replacement systems and components installed in existing dwellings, the standards represent reasonable provision for complying with the Building Regulations.

It is important to note that standards higher than many of these recommended minimum standards will need to be achieved if:

- **new dwellings are to meet the the Building Regulations target carbon dioxide emission rate (TER) calculated using SAP[1]**

- **systems are to comply with the Microgeneration Certification Scheme standards[2] that enable building owners to receive payments under the Renewable Heat Incentive (RHI) and qualify for Green Deal funding**

- **products are to be recognised as renewable technologies under the Renewable Energy Directive.**

The guide includes some supplementary information that identifies good practice design and installation standards that exceed the minimum standards in this guide. Microgeneration Certification Scheme standards are an example of good practice standards.

A summary of recommended minimum energy efficiency standards is presented in Table 1 at the end of this section.

1.2 Innovative systems

It is also important to note that this guide covers a range of frequently occurring situations and deals with the most commonly used fixed building services technologies. In doing so it neither endorses

---

1   Standard Assessment Procedure, www.bre.co.uk/SAP2012
2   http://www.microgenerationcertification.org/mcs-standards

these methods and technologies nor excludes other more innovative technologies that may offer an alternative means of meeting the functional requirements of the Building Regulations.

Where the alternative technology has been the subject of a recognised testing procedure that assesses its energy performance, this may be used to indicate that the system is adequately efficient. In the event that there is no recognised testing standard, suitable calculations or modelling methods may be used to show the carbon performance of the system.

1.3 European directives

The design and installation of fixed building services products, such as boilers, circulators and heat pumps, shall at the appropriate time comply with all relevant requirements of EU directives as implemented in the United Kingdom. There are a number of directives with requirements that directly or indirectly control the energy efficiency of building services.

The **Ecodesign Directive 2009/125/EC** provides a framework for establishing requirements for 'energy-related' products placed on the EU market. Current requirements cover 'energy-using' products such as boilers, light bulbs and washing machines. In the future, requirements will also cover products such as windows, insulation material and shower heads whose use has an impact on energy consumption.

The requirements are set out in Commission Regulations listed in the document http://ec.europa.eu/energy/efficiency/ecodesign/doc/overview_legislation_eco-design.pdf. Products covered by the regulations can only be CE marked and placed on the market if they meet the ecodesign standards specified.

At the time of preparation of this guide, Commission Regulations existed or were being developed for:

- space heaters and combination heaters
- water heaters and hot water storage tanks
- glandless standalone circulators and glandless circulators integrated in products
- water pumps
- air conditioners and comfort fans
- fans driven by motors with an electric input power between 125 W and 500 W
- lighting products in the domestic and tertiary sectors
- electric motors.

The intention is that the recommended minimum product standards in this guide should at least match the energy efficiency standards set out in Commission Regulations *as they come into force*. For example, although the implementing regulations for hot water storage tanks were published in September 2013, the standards do not come into force until September 2017.

If in any doubt as to whether a product is subject to minimum ecodesign standards, check the Commission document above.

The **Energy Labelling Directive 2010/30/EU** complements the Ecodesign Directive by providing a framework for labelling of energy-related products including lamps, luminaires, household air conditioners and washing machines. The Energy Label classifies products on an A to G scale, 'pulling' the market towards more efficient products by better informing consumers. The Ecodesign Directive, by contrast, uses regulation to 'push' the market away from the worst performing products.

The **Renewable Energy Directive 2009/28/EC** provides a framework for the promotion of energy from renewable resources. It sets a mandatory UK target of 15% energy generation from renewable sources by

2020 – the 'renewable energy obligation' – as a contribution to meeting the EU's overall target of 20%. Of relevance to building services is that the directive identifies criteria for training and certification of installers of renewables. The directive also specifies in Annex VII the standards that heat pumps must achieve to be recognised as renewable technologies by the directive.

The **Energy Efficiency Directive 2012/27/EU** establishes a common framework of measures for the promotion of energy efficiency within the EU in order to ensure that the EU meets its target of a 20% reduction in primary energy consumption by 2020. Legislation to implement the directive in the UK will be published by 5 June 2014. Included will be requirements for public authorities to purchase only energy-efficient products, services and buildings; and requirements for heat meters to be fitted in apartments and buildings connected to a central source of heating or a district heating network. For more information on the specific requirements and technical standards, see the DECC website[3].

The **Energy Performance of Buildings Directive 2010/31/EU** is a recast of the original 2002/91/EC directive, which in 2002 introduced requirements for:

- the establishment of a methodology for calculating the integrated energy performance of buildings
- minimum energy performance requirements for new buildings, and, where feasible, for larger buildings undergoing major renovation
- energy performance certification of buildings, and
- inspections of heating and air conditioning systems.

The recast directive includes a new requirement to consider in the design of new buildings the feasibility of using renewables and other 'high-efficiency alternative systems'. There is no mandatory format for this assessment, but it will now be necessary to declare (through a new field in the energy performance calculation software) that it has been carried out.

The Building Regulations, which already met the original requirements in many ways (for example by setting standards for new buildings), have been amended in some places to reflect the new requirements of the directive. For guidance on the changes affecting new dwellings, see Approved Document L1A. For guidance on the changes affecting major renovations, see Approved Document L1B. For guidance on other requirements relating to building certification and inspection of heating and air conditioning systems, see the DCLG website[4].

1.4 Status of guide

The Building Regulations contain functional requirements, such as requirements that buildings must be structurally stable, constructed and fitted to ensure fire protection, and energy efficient. These functional requirements are often drafted in broad terms, and so it may not always be immediately clear to a person carrying out work how to comply with the relevant requirements. Consequently, the Department for Communities and Local Government issues documents, known as approved documents, which provide practical guidance on ways of complying with specific aspects of the Building Regulations in some of the more common building situations.

Approved documents are not always comprehensive and may contain references to other documents which will provide more detailed information and assistance on parts of the guidance. This guide is one of those documents: it provides more detailed information on the guidance contained in Approved Documents L1A and L1B about compliance with the energy efficiency requirements which apply when installing fixed building services in new and existing dwellings.

---

3   https://www.gov.uk/decc
4   https://www.gov.uk/dclg

If you follow the relevant guidance in an approved document, and in any document referred to in the approved document (such as this guide) which provides additional information to help you follow that guidance, there is a legal presumption that you have complied with the Building Regulations. However, in each case it is for the building control body (local authority or approved inspector) to decide whether work complies with the requirements of the Building Regulations. It is therefore sensible that you check with the building control body before starting work what they consider it is necessary for you to do to comply with the requirements of the Building Regulations.

1.5 How to use this guide

The guide comprises four fuel-based sections and nine technology-specific sections:

- Fuel-based

  Section 2: Gas-fired space and water heating

  Section 3: Oil-fired space and water heating

  Section 4: Electric heating

  Section 5: Solid fuel heating

- Technology-specific

  Section 6: Community heating

  Section 7: Underfloor heating

  Section 8: Mechanical ventilation

  Section 9: Heat pumps

  Section 10: Comfort cooling

  Section 11: Solar water heating

  Section 12: Lighting

  Section 13: Micro-combined heat and power

  Section 14: Heating system circulators

For any particular application, reference may need to be made to more than one section.

Supplementary information is shown against a blue background. This may be further information to help with interpreting the minimum energy efficiency provisions needed to comply with the Building Regulations. Or it may be guidance on best practice that goes beyond the recommended minimum standards.

Key terms are printed in blue at appropriate points throughout the guide.

1.6 Key terms

Fixed building services means any part of, or any controls associated with:

a. fixed internal or external lighting systems, but does not include emergency escape lighting or specialist process lighting

b. fixed systems for heating, domestic hot water, air conditioning or mechanical ventilation, or

c. any combination of systems of the kinds referred to in sub-paragraph a. or b.

New system means a fixed building services system installed:

a.   in a new building

b.   for the first time in an existing building

c.   as a complete replacement for a system in an existing building.

Seasonal efficiency means the efficiency value used by SAP for a heating appliance. For gas, LPG and oil boilers that have been tested for efficiency, this is SEDBUK[5]. For gas boilers installed in existing buildings, this is ErP[6].

1.7 Work on existing systems

A requirement of the Building Regulations is that work on existing buildings should be carried out in such a way that when the work is complete:

a.   the work itself complies with the applicable requirements of the Building Regulations

b.   the parts of the building not affected by the work are no more unsatisfactory in relation to the requirements of the Regulations than before the work was started.

This means that when a system component like a room thermostat is replaced, only the new component is expected to comply with the standards in this guide (which in some cases may be lower than for new systems).

When replacing a boiler, the boiler controls are considered to be part of the boiler installation and should therefore meet the standards set out in the relevant sections of this document. For gas-fired combination boilers, certain energy efficiency measures are also considered to be part of the boiler installation and should meet the standards set out in Section 3.

It is not a general requirement to upgrade the rest of the existing system, but this guide does include some recommendations on minor upgrades for compliance with the Building Regulations where they would be cost-effective and may be necessary to ensure efficient operation of the new component.

Some of the supplementary information is guidance on good practice that, while not essential for compliance with the Building Regulations, would help to save energy. For example, it is convenient and timely to fit thermostatic radiator valves when replacing a boiler and the system has been drained down.

1.8 Replacement of primary heating appliances

When replacing an existing appliance, the efficiency of the new appliance should not be significantly less than the efficiency of the appliance being replaced. If the replacement involves a fuel switch, then the relative carbon emissions associated with the new and existing fuels should be considered when assessing the reasonableness of the proposed new appliance. The aim is to discourage replacement of an existing appliance by a significantly less carbon efficient one.

For gas-fired boilers[7], a minimum energy efficiency standard applies to the replacement appliance. For gas and oil-fired boilers, the installation of a replacement appliance should also include adequate controls. For gas-fired combination boilers, the installation of a replacement appliance should also include additional energy efficiency measures. Full details of these requirements can be found in Section 2 for gas-fired boilers and Section 3 for oil-fired boilers.

---

5   The SAP Product Characteristics Database (PCDB) at www.ncm-pcdb.org.uk/sap displays separate SAP winter and summer seasonal efficiencies for boilers held within it. SAP 2012 (available at www.bre.co.uk/sap2012) uses these values to calculate the carbon dioxide emission rate for a dwelling. SAP winter and summer seasonal efficiencies are derived from SEDBUK 2009 values.

6   Refers to the efficiency methodology set out in Directive 2009/125/EC for energy performance related products.

7   Except heating boilers that are combined with range cookers.

Replacement not involving fuel or energy switch

Where the primary heating appliance is replaced by one using the same fuel or energy supply, the seasonal efficiency of the new equipment should be:

a. as stated in the relevant fuel-based section of this guide, and

b. not worse than 2 percentage points lower than the seasonal efficiency of the controlled service being replaced. If the efficiency of the appliance to be replaced is not known, efficiency values may be taken from Table 4a or 4b of SAP 2012.

Replacement involving fuel or energy switch

If the new heating appliance uses a different fuel, the efficiency of the new service should be multiplied by the ratio of the carbon dioxide emission factor of the fuel used in the service being replaced to that of the fuel used in the new service, to obtain the 'carbon equivalent efficiency'. The checks described in sub-paragraphs a. and b. above should then be made. The carbon dioxide emission factors should be taken from Table 12 of SAP 2012.

Electric flow boilers

It will not normally be possible to replace a gas boiler with an electric flow boiler and meet the standard above for replacements involving an energy switch. However, if it is not practicable or permissible to fit a replacement gas boiler in a dwelling – for example because the boiler installation would not comply with relevant British Standards or the Building Regulations, or listed building consent has not been granted to install a new flue or gas supply – then, provided there is no possible alternative, fitting an electric flow boiler in accordance with the guidance on electric heating systems in Section 4 of this guide would be acceptable, and count as making 'reasonable provision' for the purposes of complying with the requirements of the Building Regulations.

Example

An old oil-fired boiler with a seasonal efficiency of 72% is to be replaced by a dual solid fuel boiler. The new dual solid fuel boiler should have:

a. a seasonal efficiency not less than 65% (from Table 21 in this guide), and

b. a carbon equivalent efficiency not less than 70%.

A dual solid fuel boiler with a seasonal efficiency of 65% will meet condition b. as its carbon equivalent efficiency is:

$$65\% \times (0.298 \div 0.226) = 85.7\%$$

where 0.298 and 0.226 $kgCO_2/kWh$ are the emission factors for oil and dual solid fuels respectively.

1.9 Summary of recommended minimum energy efficiency standards

Table 1 Recommended minimum energy efficiency standards for building services[8]

Gas-fired wet central heating	Seasonal efficiency		
	SEDBUK 2009[9]	SEDBUK 2005/ SEDBUK	ErP[10]
Condensing boilers in new dwellings	88%	90%	-
Condensing boilers in existing dwellings	-	-	92%
Non-condensing boilers (where permitted): natural gas/LPG	78%/80%	78%/80%	-
Range cooker boilers	75%	75%	-
Gas-fired warm air heating	**Efficiency**		
	See Table 6		
Gas-fired fixed independent space heaters	**Efficiency (gross)[11]**		
Gas and LPG primary heating	63%		
Gas and LPG secondary heating	63% (new build) 45% (existing build)		
Decorative fuel-effect	Not specified (set to 20% in SAP 2012)		
Gas fires in combined fire/backboilers (replacements)	**Efficiency (gross)**		
	Natural gas	**LPG**	
Inset live fuel-effect	45%	46%	
All types except inset live fuel-effect	63%	64%	
Oil-fired wet central heating	**Seasonal efficiency**		
	SEDBUK 2009	**SEDBUK 2005/SEDBUK**	
Condensing regular boilers	88%	90%	
Condensing combination boilers	86%	86%	
Non-condensing regular boilers (where permitted)	84%	85%	
Non-condensing combination boilers (where permitted)	82%	82%	
Range cooker boilers	80%	80%	
Oil-fired appliances	**Efficiency (gross)**		
Continuously-burning vaporising for secondary heating or hot water	See Section 3.4		
Fixed independent for primary and secondary space heating	60%		
Electric heating	**Efficiency**		
Boilers serving central heating	N/A		
Warm air	N/A		

8 Emerging European regulations implementing the Ecodesign Directive will set minimum standards for the efficiency of energy-using products that can be placed on the market. Products should also comply with these standards as they come into effect. Current regulations are listed at http://ec.europa.eu/energy/efficiency/ecodesign/doc/overview_legislation_eco-design.pdf.

9 Seasonal Efficiency of Domestic Boilers in the UK (SEDBUK). The boiler efficiency should meet either the SEDBUK 2009 or SEDBUK 2005 standard. If the SEDBUK efficiency in a boiler manufacturer's literature does not state whether it is SEDBUK 2009 or SEDBUK 2005, it should be assumed to be SEDBUK 2005.

10 Refers to the efficiency methodology set out in Directive 2009/125/EC for energy performance related products.

11 Efficiency is heat output divided by calorific value of fuel. The net calorific value of a fuel excludes the latent heat of water vapour in the exhaust, and so is lower than the gross calorific value. European standards normally use net calorific values while SAP 2012 uses gross values. SAP Table E4 gives factors for converting net efficiency to gross efficiency.

Table 1 Recommended minimum energy efficiency standards for building services *(continued)*

Panel heaters		N/A	
Storage, including integrated storage/direct		N/A	
Solid fuel heating		**Efficiency (gross)**	**Feed**
B1	Simple open fire – inset	37%	Batch
B2	Open fire – freestanding convector	47%	Batch
B3	Open fire inset convector	45% mineral fuels 43% wood fuels	
C1/2	Open fire and boiler (inset or freestanding)	50%	Batch
D1/2/3	Open fire + high output boiler (trapezium and rectangular grates)	63%	Batch
D4	Open fire + high output boiler (rectangle)	63%	Batch
E 1	Dry room heater (dry stove)	65%	Batch/auto
E 2	Dry room heater – wood logs only	65%	Batch
E 3	Dry room heater – multi-fuel	65%	Batch
E 4	Dry room heater – pellet stove	65% part load 70% nominal load	Auto
F	Room heater with boiler	67% mineral fuels and wood logs 70% wood pellets – part load 75% wood pellets – nominal load	Batch/auto
G1	Cooker without boiler not exceeding 3.5 kW	65% mineral fuels 55% wood fuels	Batch
G2	Cooker with heating boiler exceeding 3.5 kW	65% mineral fuels 60% wood fuels	Batch
J2	Independent boiler – wood logs only	75%	Batch
J3	Independent boiler – multi-fuel	65% mineral fuels 75% wood logs	Batch
J4	Independent boiler – anthracite	70% up to 20.5 kW 75% above 20.5 kW	Auto
J5	Independent boiler – wood/pellets/chips	75% nominal load 70% part load	Auto
	Slow heat release appliances	65%	Batch
	One-off tiled/mortared stoves	70%	Batch
Community heating		**Seasonal efficiency**	
Boilers		See *Non-Domestic Building Services Compliance Guide*	

Table 1 Recommended minimum energy efficiency standards for building services (continued)

Mechanical ventilation	Specific fan power (SFP) (W/(l·s))	
Intermittent extract	0.5	
Continuous extract	0.7	
Continuous supply	0.5	
Continuous supply and extract with heat recovery	1.5	

Heat recovery	Dry heat recovery efficiency	
Balanced mechanical ventilation systems	70%	

Heat pumps – electrically driven	Coefficient of performance (COP)	
	New build[12]	Existing build
Air-to-air	Space heating ≤12 kW	Seasonal COP 'D' rating for the median temperature range in BS EN 14825[13]	
All others	Space heating	2.5 at rating conditions in BS EN 14511[14]	2.2 at rating conditions in BS EN 14511
	Domestic hot water	2.0 at rating conditions in BS EN 14511	

Comfort cooling	Energy efficiency ratio (EER)	
Air-cooled air conditioners working in cooling mode	2.4	
Water-cooled air conditioners working in cooling mode	2.5	
Fixed air conditioners	> Class C in Schedule 3 of the labelling scheme (The Energy Information (Household Air Conditioners) (No 2) Regulations, SI 2005/1726)	

Solar water heating	Circulation pump power	
	< 50 W < 2% of peak thermal power of collector	

Fixed lighting	Lighting efficacy	
Internal light fittings (75%)	45 lamp lumens per circuit-watt	
External lighting – automatic presence and daylight control	Lamp capacity < 100 lamp-watts per light fitting	
External lighting – manual switching and automatic daylight control	45 lumens per circuit-watt	

Micro-CHP	Heating plant emission rate (HPER)	
	See Section 13.3 a	

Heating system circulators	Energy Efficiency Index	
Glandless standalone Glandless, standalone and integrated	≤0.27 until 31 July 2015 ≤0.23 from 1 August 2015	

12 SAP 2012 calculations use the heat pump seasonal performance factor (SPF) – either measured values for products listed in the Product Characteristics Database, or the default values in Table 4a for products not listed.

13 Seasonal coefficient of performance (SCOP) is the current Ecodesign Directive measure for space heating air-to-air heat pumps with an output of up to 12 kW. Eventually, the measure used will be the seasonal primary energy efficiency ratio (SPEER), with testing and rating to BS EN 14825:2013 *Air conditioners, liquid chilling packages and heat pumps with electrically driven compressors for space heating and cooling. Testing and rating at part load conditions and calculation of seasonal performance.* Energy labelling with the SPEER rating will be mandatory from 2015.

14 Rating conditions are standardised conditions for determining performance specified in BS EN 14511:2013 *Air conditioners, liquid chilling packages and heat pumps with electrically driven compressors for space heating and cooling.*

Section 2: Gas-fired space and water heating

2.1 Scope of guidance

This section provides guidance on the specification of gas-fired space heating and hot water systems[15] in dwellings to meet relevant energy efficiency requirements in the Building Regulations. The guidance applies to systems fuelled by natural gas and liquid petroleum gas (LPG) and covers:

- wet central heating systems
- range cookers with integral central heating boilers
- warm air heating systems
- fixed independent space heating devices.

2.2 Key terms

Flue gas heat recovery means a device which pre-heats the domestic hot water supply by recovering heat from the boiler's flue emissions.

Weather compensation means a control function which maintains internal temperatures by varying the flow temperature from the heat generator relative to the measured outside air temperature.

Load compensation means a control function which maintains internal temperatures by varying the flow temperature from the heat generator relative to the measured response of the heating system.

Automation means a control function which automatically adjusts time and temperature settings based on occupancy detection and/or stored data from user adjustments over time.

Optimisation means a control function which starts the boiler operation at the optimum time to achieve the setpoint temperature at the start of the occupancy period.

2.3 Gas-fired wet central heating systems

New systems

New systems for gas-fired wet central heating in new and existing dwellings should meet the minimum standards for:

a. boiler efficiency, system circulation, hot water storage, system preparation and commissioning in Table 2

b. boiler interlock, zoning, and time and temperature control of the heating and hot water circuits in Table 3

c. pipework insulation in Table 5.

Work in existing buildings

Components installed as replacements in existing systems should meet the same standards as for new systems, except where indicated otherwise in Table 4.

Where a new or replacement gas-fired boiler is installed in an existing dwelling, both of the following minimum standards should be met:

a. boiler efficiency, in Table 2

---

15   All gas appliances must be installed by a competent person in accordance with the current issue of the Gas Safety (Installation and Use) Regulations. The installation should follow the manufacturer's instructions and should comply with all relevant parts of the Building Regulations and, for wet systems, the Water Regulations.

b. boiler interlock, time and temperature control.

If the new or replacement gas-fired boiler is a combination boiler, the following standard should also be met:

c. at least one of the energy efficiency measures in the 'Minimum standard' column of Table 4, section 2.0.

Table 4 lists minimum standards when replacing components of gas-fired wet central heating systems. Table 4 in addition identifies good practice upgrades to the rest of the system (beyond the requirements of the Building Regulations) when making planned and emergency replacements.

Table 2 Recommended minimum standards for efficiency, system circulation, hot water storage, system preparation and commissioning for gas-fired wet central heating systems

	Minimum standard	Supplementary information
1.0 Efficiency	a. The boiler SEDBUK 2009 efficiency for boilers in new dwellings should not be less than 88%. b. The boiler ErP efficiency for boilers installed in existing dwellings should not be less than 92%. c. In existing dwellings, in the exceptional circumstances defined in the DCLG *Guide to the condensing boiler installation assessment procedure for dwellings*[16], the ErP efficiency standard would not apply and instead the boiler SEDBUK 2009 efficiency should not be less than 78% if natural gas-fired, or not less than 80% if LPG-fired. d. The boiler efficiency for heating boilers that are combined with range cookers should be as defined in Section 2.3.	The SAP Product Characteristics Database (PCDB) at www.ncm-pcdb.org.uk/sap displays separate SAP winter and summer seasonal efficiencies for boilers held within it. SAP 2012 (available at www.bre.co.uk/sap2012) uses these values to calculate the carbon dioxide emission rate for a dwelling. SAP winter and summer seasonal efficiencies are derived from SEDBUK 2009 values. SEDBUK 2009 and SEDBUK 2005 efficiency values are different to one another, and both are different to the ErP efficiency. If the SEDBUK efficiency in a boiler manufacturer's literature does not state whether it is SEDBUK 2009 or SEDBUK 2005, it should be assumed to be SEDBUK 2005. Minimum SEDBUK 2005 efficiency values for boilers are set out in Table 1 and in the 2010 edition of this guide All boiler manufacturers should be calculating and declaring the energy efficiency of boilers in line with the ERP methodology. For boilers installed in existing buildings, the ErP efficiency should be used and not the SEDBUK efficiency values. The DCLG *Guide to the condensing boiler installation assessment procedure for dwellings* sets out the approved procedure for establishing the exceptional circumstances in which boilers may be of the non-condensing type. Systems with condensing boilers should be designed to have low primary return water temperatures, preferably less than 55°C, to maximise condensing operation. Low return water temperatures can be obtained through techniques such as weather compensation and the use of low temperature heat emitters (for example correctly-sized radiators and underfloor heating elements). Low temperature heat emitters will also be compatible with low temperature heat generators, such as heat pumps, that might be installed as replacements in the future.

---

16   *Guide to the condensing boiler installation assessment procedure for dwellings*, ODPM, 2005.

Table 2 Recommended minimum standards for efficiency, system circulation, hot water storage, system preparation and commissioning for gas-fired wet central heating systems *(continued)*

	Minimum standard	Supplementary information
2.0 System circulation	a. Space heating systems and domestic hot water primary circuits should have fully pumped circulation. b. If the boiler manufacturer's instructions advise installation of a bypass, an automatic bypass valve should be provided and the manufacturer's instructions on minimum pipe length followed.	

3.0 Hot water storage	a. Vented copper hot water storage cylinders should comply with the heat loss and heat exchanger requirements of BS 1566:2002 Part 1.
	
	b. Copper hot water storage combination units should comply with BS 3198:1981.
	
	c. Primary storage systems should meet the insulation requirements of the Hot Water Association *Performance specification for thermal stores*.
	
	d. Unvented hot water storage system products should comply with BS EN 12897:2006 or an equivalent standard.
	
	e. The standing heat loss for all hot water storage vessels in a., b., c. and d. above should not exceed $Q = 1.15 \times (0.2 + 0.051V^{2/3})$ kWh/day, where V is the volume of the cylinder in litres.
	
	f. All hot water vessels should carry a label with the following information:
	
	  i. type of vessel (vented, unvented, combination unit or thermal store)
	
	  ii. nominal capacity in litres
	
	  iii. standing heat loss in kWh/day
	
	  iv. heat exchanger performance in kW
	
	  v. reference to product compliance with relevant standard (e.g. BS 1566, BS EN 12897) and logos of accreditation bodies as required.
	
	For labelling requirements for other heat inputs, see relevant sections (e.g. Section 11 for solar).
		If a vented cylinder is not made from copper then the heat loss and heat exchange characteristics should be tested in accordance with BS EN 12897:2006.
		
		The HWA thermal storage specification is available for free download from www.hotwater.org.uk.
		
		British Standards
		
		BS 1566-1:2002 *Copper indirect cylinders for domestic purposes. Open vented copper cylinders. Requirements and test methods.*
		
		BS EN 12897:2006 *Water supply. Specification for indirectly heated unvented (closed) storage water heaters.*
		
		BS 3198:1981 *Copper hot water storage combination units for domestic purposes.*

Table 2 Recommended minimum standards for efficiency, system circulation, hot water storage, system preparation and commissioning for gas-fired wet central heating systems *(continued)*

	Minimum standard	Supplementary information
4.0 System preparation and water treatment	a. Central heating systems should be thoroughly cleaned and flushed out before installing a new boiler. b. During final filling of the system, a chemical water treatment inhibitor meeting the manufacturer's specification or other appropriate standard should be added to the primary circuit to control corrosion and the formation of scale and sludge. c. Installers should also refer to the boiler manufacturer's installation instructions for appropriate treatment products and special requirements for individual boiler models. d. Where the mains total water hardness exceeds 200 parts per million, provision should be made to treat the feed water to water heaters and the hot water circuit of combination boilers to reduce the rate of accumulation of limescale. e. For solar thermal systems, see Section 11.	Inhibitors should be BuildCert approved or equivalent. Limescale can be controlled by the use of chemical limescale inhibitors, combined corrosion and limescale inhibitors, polyphosphate dosing, electrolytic scale reducers or water softeners. The relevant standard for water treatment is BS 7593:2006 *Code of practice for treatment of water in domestic hot water central heating systems*. BS 7593 notes that "naturally soft waters of low alkalinity or those supplied via a base-exchange resin softener have an increased potential for corrosion, and, if they are used in any central heating system, a corrosion inhibitor specifically formulated for the purpose should be added and properly maintained." Manufacturers should be consulted for advice, paying particular attention to dosage levels. Special radiator valves are available that will seal off the radiator as well as the heating circuit to prevent loss of inhibitor when removing a radiator for service or maintenance. A filter can also be fitted to the central heating circuit to help maintain the efficiency and reliability of the system.
5.0 Commiss-ioning	a. On completion of the installation of a boiler or hot water storage system and associated equipment such as pipework, pumps and controls, the equipment should be commissioned in accordance with the manufacturer's instructions. These instructions will be specific to the particular boiler or hot water storage system. b. The installer should explain fully to the user how to operate the system in an energy efficient manner, and leave behind any user manuals provided by manufacturers.	**The Benchmark System** The Benchmark Commissioning Checklist can be used to show that commissioning has been carried out satisfactorily. Benchmark licence-holders provide a checklist with the appliance for completion by the persons commissioning the system so that they can record that all the checks have been made and the results show efficient operation of the equipment in compliance with the Building Regulations. The Benchmark checklist should be provided to the builder, or the householder in the case of work in existing dwellings, an appointed agent, or the end user. A Benchmark Commissioning Checklist will be included in all HHIC gas boiler manufacturer members' installation manuals to help installers record information about the installation in order to assist with servicing and repairs. For example, details of system cleaners and inhibitors can be recorded. Only manufacturing companies who hold a Benchmark licence will be eligible to use the Benchmark logo and the approved log book wording and layout. (Benchmark is registered as a European Collective Mark by the Heating and Hot Water Industry Council, and the content is copyright.)

Table 3 Recommended minimum controls for new gas-fired wet central heating systems[1][2]

Control type	Minimum standard
1.0 Boiler interlock	a. System controls should be wired so that when there is no demand for space heating or hot water, the boiler and pump are switched off.
2.0 Zoning	a. Dwellings with a total floor area > 150 m² should have at least two space heating zones, each with an independently controlled heating circuit[3].
	b. Dwellings with a total floor area[4] ≤ 150 m² may have a single space heating zone[5].
3.0 Control of space heating	a. Each space heating circuit should be provided with:
	i. independent time control, and either:
	ii. a room thermostat or programmable room thermostat located in a reference room[6] served by the heating circuit, together with individual radiator controls such as thermostatic radiator valves (TRVs) on all radiators outside the reference rooms, or
	iii. individual networked radiator controls in each room on the circuit.
4.0 Control of hot water	a. Domestic hot water circuits supplied from a hot water store (i.e. not produced instantaneously as by a combination boiler) should be provided with:
	i. independent time control, and
	ii. electric temperature control using, for example, a cylinder thermostat and a zone valve or three-port valve. (If the use of a zone valve is not appropriate, as with thermal stores, a second pump could be substituted for the zone valve.)

Notes
[1] The standards in this table apply to new gas-fired wet central heating systems. In existing dwellings, the standards set out in Table 4 will apply in addition.
[2] Always also follow manufacturers' instructions.
[3] A heating circuit refers to a pipework run serving a number of radiators that is controlled by its own zone valve.
[4] The relevant floor area is the area within the insulated envelope of the dwelling, including internal cupboards and stairwells.
[5] The SAP notional dwelling assumes at least two space heating zones for all floor areas, unless the dwelling is single storey, open plan with a living area > 70% of the total floor area.
[6] A reference room is a room that will act as the main temperature control for the whole circuit and where no other form of system temperature control is present.

Table 4 Recommended minimum standards when replacing components of gas-fired wet central heating systems[1]

Component	Reason	Minimum standard	Good practice[2]
1.0 Hot water cylinder	Emergency	a. For copper vented cylinders and combination units, the standing losses should not exceed $Q = 1.28 \times (0.2 + 0.051V^{2/3})$ kWh/day, where V is the volume of the cylinder in litres.	a. Upgrade gravity-fed systems to fully pumped.
		b. Install an electric temperature control, such as a cylinder thermostat. Where the cylinder or installation is of a type that precludes the fitting of wired controls, install either a wireless or thermo-mechanical hot water cylinder thermostat or electric temperature control.	b. Install a boiler interlock and separate timing for space heating and hot water.
		c. If separate time control for the heating circuit is not present, use of single time control for space heating and hot water is acceptable.	

Table 4 Recommended minimum standards when replacing components of gas-fired wet central heating systems (continued)[1]

Component	Reason	Minimum standard	Good practice[2]
	Planned	d. Install a boiler interlock and separate timing for space heating and hot water.	c. Upgrade gravity-fed systems to fully pumped.
2.0 Boiler	Emergency/planned	**All boiler types except heating boilers that are combined with range cookers** a. The ErP[3] seasonal efficiency of the boiler should be a minimum of 92% and not significantly less than the efficiency of the appliance being replaced – as set out in paragraph 1.8. b. In the exceptional circumstances defined in the *Guide to the condensing boiler installation assessment procedure for dwellings*[4], the boiler SEDBUK 2009 efficiency should not be less than 78% if natural gas-fired, or not less than 80% if LPG-fired. In these circumstances the additional requirements for combination boilers would not apply. c. Install a boiler interlock as defined for new systems. d. Time and temperature control should be installed for the heating system. **Combination boilers** e. In addition to the above, at least one of the following energy efficiency measures should be installed. The measure(s) chosen should be appropriate to the system in which it is installed: i. Flue gas heat recovery. ii. Weather compensation. iii. Load compensation. iv. Smart thermostat with automation and optimisation.	a. Upgrade gravity-fed systems to fully pumped. b. Fit individual radiator controls such as thermostatic radiator valves (TRVs) on all radiators except those in the reference room.
3.0 Radiator	Emergency		a. Fit a TRV to the replacement radiator if in a room without a room thermostat.
	Planned		b. Fit TRVs to all radiators in rooms without a room thermostat.
4.0 New heating system – existing pipework retained	Planned	a. The new boiler and its controls should meet the standards in section 2.0 of this table. b. Fit individual radiator controls such as TRVs on all radiators except those in the reference room.	a. In dwellings with a total floor area > 150 m², install at least two heating circuits, each with independent time and temperature control, together with individual radiator controls such as TRVs on all radiators except those in the reference rooms.

Notes
[1] Always also follow manufacturers' instructions.
[2] Best practice would be as for a new system.
[3] Refers to the efficiency methodology set out in Directive 2009/125/EC for energy performance related products.
[4] *Guide to the condensing boiler installation assessment procedure for dwellings*, ODPM, 2005.

Table 5 Recommended minimum standards for insulation of pipework in gas-fired wet central heating systems

Minimum standard

a. Pipes should be insulated to comply with the maximum permissible heat loss indicated in the Supplementary information column, and labelled accordingly, as follows:

i. Primary circulation pipes for heating circuits should be insulated wherever they pass outside the heated living space or through voids which communicate with and are ventilated from unheated spaces.

ii. Primary circulation pipes for domestic hot water circuits should be insulated throughout their length, subject only to practical constraints imposed by the need to penetrate joists and other structural elements.

iii. All pipes connected to hot water storage vessels, including the vent pipe, should be insulated for at least 1 metre from their points of connection to the cylinder (or they should be insulated up to the point where they become concealed).

iv. If secondary circulation is used, all pipes kept hot by that circulation should be insulated.

b. Whenever a boiler or hot water storage vessel is replaced in an existing system, any pipes that are exposed as part of the work or are otherwise accessible should be insulated as recommended above – or to some lesser standard where practical constraints dictate.

Supplementary information

Pipe outside diameter (mm)	Maximum heat loss (W/m)
8	7.06
10	7.23
12	7.35
15	7.89
22	9.12
28	10.07
35	11.08
42	12.19
54	14.12

In assessing the thickness of insulation required, standardised conditions should be assumed in all compliance calculations, based on a horizontal pipe at 60°C in still air at 15°C.

Further guidance on converting heat loss limits to insulation thickness for specific thermal conductivities is available in TIMSA *HVAC guidance for achieving compliance with Part L of the Building Regulations*.

Insulation of pipework in unheated areas
It may be necessary to protect central heating and hot water pipework in unheated areas against freezing. Guidance is available in:

- BS 5422:2009 *Method for specifying thermal insulating materials for pipes, tanks, vessels, ductwork and equipment operating within the temperature range -40°C to +700°C*.

- BRE Report No 262 *Thermal insulation: avoiding risks*, 2002 edition.

2.4 Gas-fired range cookers with integral central heating boiler

Note: This section does not apply to appliances with fully independent boiler and cooker parts within a shared case. For these, the standards for the boiler are as set out in Section 2.3.

Where gas-fired range cookers with an integral central heating boiler (within a single appliance body) are provided as part of a new system or as a replacement component:

a. The appliance should have two independently controlled burners (one for the cooking function and one for the boiler).

b. The SEDBUK 2009 efficiency of the integral boiler should not be less than 75%. The manufacturer's declaration of appliance performance and SEDBUK value should include the following words:

   i. *Seasonal efficiency (SEDBUK) = xx %*

   ii. *Case heat emission value = yy kW*

   iii. *Heat transfer to water at full load = zz kW*

   iv. *The values are used in the UK Government's Standard Assessment Procedure (SAP) for the energy rating of dwellings. The test data from which the values have been calculated has been certified by {insert name and/or identification of Notified Body}. See: www.rangeefficiency.org.uk.*

   If the integral boiler is a condensing boiler, the declaration should make clear whether the efficiency has been calculated in accordance with SEDBUK 2005 or SEDBUK 2009. If it does not, then SEDBUK 2005 must be assumed.

c. The integral boiler should meet the minimum standards for system circulation, hot water storage, system preparation, commissioning, controls and insulation in Tables 2, 3 and 5 (gas-fired central heating systems).

2.5 Gas-fired warm air heating

New systems and replacement components for gas-fired warm air heating should meet the minimum standards for:

a. efficiency and installation in Table 6

b. zoning, time control and temperature control for (a) space heating without hot water and (b) space heating combined with water heating in Table 7.

Table 6 Recommended minimum standards for efficiency and installation of gas-fired warm air heating systems

	Minimum standard	Supplementary information
1.0 Efficiency	a. Gas-fired warm air units should meet the requirements, as appropriate to the design of the appliance, of: i. BS EN 778:2009, or ii. BS EN 1319:2009. b. If a gas-fired circulator is incorporated in the warm air unit to provide domestic hot water, it should be able to deliver full and part load efficiency at least equal to that prescribed by BS EN 483:1999+A4:2007. c. The manufacturer's declaration of appliance performance should include the following words: i. **Combined warm air unit and circulator** *This product has been assessed against the test methods set out in BS EN 778:2009/BS EN 1319:2009/BS EN 483* and certified as meeting those minimum requirements by {insert name and/or identification of Notified Body}.* ii. **Warm air unit alone** *This product has been assessed against the test method set out in BS EN 778:2009/ BS EN 1319:2009* and certified as meeting the minimum requirements by {insert name and/or identification of Notified Body}.* *Delete as appropriate	**British Standards** BS EN 778:2009 *Domestic gas-fired forced convection air heaters for space heating not exceeding a net heat input of 70 kW, without a fan to assist transportation of combustion air and/or combustion products.* BS EN 1319:2009 *Domestic gas-fired forced convection air heaters for space heating, with fan-assisted burners not exceeding a net heat input of 70 kW.* BS EN 483:1999+A4:2007 *Gas-fired central heating boilers. Type C boilers of nominal heat input not exceeding 70 kW.*
2.0 Installation	a. The system should be installed in accordance with BS 5864:2010. b. Ductwork that is newly installed or replaced should be insulated in accordance with the recommendations of BS 5422:2009.	BS 5864:2010 *Installation and maintenance of gas-fired ducted air heaters of rated input not exceeding 70 kW net (second and third family gases). Specification.* BS 5422:2009 *Method for specifying thermal insulating materials for pipes, tanks, vessels, ductwork and equipment operating within the temperature range -40°C to +700°C.*

Table 7 Recommended minimum controls for gas-fired warm air heating systems

(a) Without hot water	Minimum standard
1.0 **Time and temperature control**	a. Where controls are external to the heater, the system should be provided with a time switch/programmer and room thermostat, or programmable room thermostat. b. Where controls are integrated in the heater, the system should be provided with a time switch/programmer and room temperature sensor linked to heater firing and fan speed control.
2.0 **Zoning**	a. Dwellings with a total floor area ≤ 150 m² should be divided into at least two space heating zones with independent temperature controls, one of which is assigned to the living area. b. Dwellings with a total floor area > 150 m² should be provided with at least two space heating zones with independent time and temperature controls.
(b) With hot water	
1.0 **System circulation**	a. There should be pumped primary circulation to the hot water cylinder.
2.0 **Time and temperature control**	a. The space heating and hot water circuits should be provided with independent time control. b. Independent temperature control of the hot water circuit should be implemented with a cylinder thermostat and a timing device, wired such that when there is no demand for hot water both the pump and circulator are switched off.
3.0 **Zoning**	a. Dwellings with a total floor area ≤ 150 m² should have at least two space heating zones with independent time controls, one of which is assigned to the living area. b. Dwellings with a total floor area > 150 m² should have at least two space heating zones with independent time and temperature controls.

2.6 Gas-fired fixed independent space heating appliances

Fixed independent space heating appliances may be installed as a means of primary or secondary space heating.

Gas-fired fixed independent appliances for primary space heating

Where gas-fired fixed independent space heating appliances in new and existing dwellings are provided as the primary heat source:

a. The appliance should be one of the types described in Table 8.

b. The efficiency of the appliance (gross calorific value) should not be less than 63% (70% net).

c. The appliance manufacturer's declaration of appliance performance should include the following words:

The efficiency of this appliance has been measured as specified in {insert appropriate entry from Table 8} and the result after conversion to gross using the appropriate factor from Table E4 of SAP 2012 is [x]%. The test data has been certified by {insert name and/or identification of Notified Body}. The gross efficiency value may be used in the UK Government's Standard Assessment Procedure (SAP) for energy rating of dwellings.

d. In new dwellings, each appliance should be capable, either independently or in conjunction with room thermostats or other suitable temperature sensing devices, of controlling the temperatures independently in areas that have different heating needs (e.g. separate sleeping and living areas). In existing dwellings, wherever practical, temperature controls should be upgraded to the standards required for new dwellings.

Table 8 Acceptable types of natural gas and LPG-fired fixed independent appliance for primary space heating

British Standard designation (appliance type)
BS EN 1266:2002 *Independent gas-fired convection heaters incorporating a fan to assist transportation of combustion air and/or flue gases.*
BS 7977-1:2009+A1:2013 *Specification for safety and rational use of energy of domestic gas appliances. Radiant/convectors.*
BS EN 613:2001 *Independent gas-fired convection heaters.*
BS EN 13278:2013 *Open fronted gas-fired independent space heaters.*

Gas-fired fixed independent appliances for secondary space heating

Where gas-fired fixed independent space heating appliances are provided as the secondary heat source:

a. In new dwellings, the appliance efficiency (gross calorific value) should not be less than 63% (70% net).

b. In existing dwellings, the appliance efficiency (gross calorific value) should not be less than 45% (50% net).

c. The appliance manufacturer's declaration of appliance performance should include the following words:

The efficiency of this appliance has been measured as specified in {insert appropriate entry from Table 9} and the result after conversion to gross using the appropriate factor from Table E4 of SAP 2012 is [x]%. The test data has been certified by {insert name and/or identification of Notified Body}. The efficiency value may be used in the UK Government's Standard Assessment Procedure (SAP) for energy rating of dwellings.

Table 9 Acceptable types of natural gas and LPG-fired fixed independent appliance for secondary space heating

BS EN 1266:2002 *Independent gas-fired convection heaters incorporating a fan to assist transportation of combustion air and/or flue gases.*	
BS 7977-1:2009+A1:2013 *Specification for safety and rational use of energy of domestic gas appliances. Radiant/convectors.*	
BS EN 613:2001 *Independent gas-fired convection heaters.*	
BS EN 13278:2013 *Open fronted gas-fired independent space heaters.*	
Flueless BS EN 14829:2007 *Independent gas-fired flueless space heaters for nominal heat input not exceeding 6 kW.* BS EN 449:2002+A1:2007 *Specification for dedicated liquefied petroleum gas appliances. Domestic flueless space heaters (including diffusive catalytic combustion heaters).*	Thermal efficiency requirements for this type of appliance are not specified as all the heat produced by the combustion process is released into the space to be heated. In SAP 2012 the efficiency of these appliances is classed as 90% and an adjustment is made for ventilation in the space heating requirement calculation.

2.7 Gas-fired fixed decorative fuel-effect fires

This type of appliance is intended for decorative purposes and therefore a minimum thermal efficiency is not specified. Note that for the purposes of SAP 2012 the efficiency of decorative fuel-effect fires is classed as 20% in the space heating requirement calculation. See Table 4a of SAP 2012.

Gas-fired decorative fires in new and existing dwellings should:

a. meet the product standards in BS EN 509:2000 *Decorative fuel-effect gas appliances*

b. number not more than one appliance per 100 m² of dwelling floor area.

2.8 Gas fires for secondary space heating provided as part of a combined fire and back boiler unit

Where gas fires are provided as a secondary heat source as part of a combined fire and back boiler unit in an existing system:

a. The appliance should be one of the types described in Table 10.

b. The efficiency (gross calorific value) of the appliance should not be less than the value in Table 10 for that type of appliance.

c. The appliance manufacturer's declaration of appliance performance should include the following words:

> *The efficiency of this appliance has been measured as specified in {insert appropriate entry from Table 10} and the result after conversion to gross using the appropriate factor from Table E4 of SAP 2012 is [x]%. The test data from which it has been calculated has been certified by {insert name and/or identification of Notified Body}. The efficiency value may be used in the UK Government's Standard Assessment Procedure (SAP) for energy rating of dwellings.*

Table 10 Minimum appliance efficiencies for gas fires in a combined fire and back boiler unit

British Standard designation (appliance type)	Minimum efficiency % (gross calorific value)	
	Natural gas	LPG
Inset live fuel-effect BS 7977-2:2003 *Specification for safety and rational use of energy of domestic gas appliances. Combined appliances. Gas fire/back boiler.*	45	46
All types except inset live fuel-effect BS 7977-2:2003 *Specification for safety and rational use of energy of domestic gas appliances. Combined appliances. Gas fire/back boiler.*	63	64

Supplementary information

Energy Efficiency Best Practice in Housing

CE30 *Domestic heating by gas: boiler systems.*

CE51 *Central heating system specifications (CHeSS).*

CE54 *Whole house boiler sizing method for houses and flats.*

SBGI publications on gas boilers and gas fires

See www.sbgi.org.uk.

CORGI Domestic Manual Series

GID1 *Essential gas safety.*

GID2 *Gas cookers and ranges.*

GID3 *Gas fires and space heaters.*

GID5 *Water heaters.*

GID7 *Central heating wet and dry.*

CORGI Design Guides

WCH1 *Wet central heating system design guide.*

WAH1 *Warm air heating system design guide.*

British Standards

BS 5440-1:2008 *Flueing and ventilation for gas appliances of rated input not exceeding 70 kW net (1st, 2nd and 3rd family gases). Specification for installation of gas appliances to chimneys and for maintenance of chimneys.*

BS 5440-2:2009 *Flueing and ventilation for gas appliances of rated input not exceeding 70 kW net (1st, 2nd and 3rd family gases). Specification for the installation and maintenance of ventilation provision for gas appliances.*

BS EN 12828:2012 *Heating systems in buildings. Design for water-based heating systems.*

BS EN 12831:2003 *Heating systems in buildings. Method for calculation of the design heat load.*

BS EN 14336:2004 *Heating systems in buildings. Installation and commissioning of water-based heating systems.*

BS 6798:2009 *Specification for installation and maintenance of gas-fired boilers of rated input not exceeding 70 kW net.*

BS 5871-1:2007 *Specification for the installation and maintenance of gas fires, convector heaters, fire/back boilers and decorative fuel effect gas appliances. Gas fires, convector heaters, fire/back boilers and heating stoves (2nd and 3rd family gases).*

BS 5871-2:2005 *Specification for the installation and maintenance of gas fires, convector heaters, fire/back boilers and decorative fuel effect gas appliances. Inset live fuel effect gas fires of heat input not exceeding 15 kW, and fire/back boilers (2nd and 3rd family gases).*

BS 5871-3:2005 *Specification for the installation and maintenance of gas fires, convector heaters, fire/back boilers and decorative fuel effect gas appliances. Decorative fuel effect gas appliances of heat input not exceeding 20 kW (2nd and 3rd family gases).*

BS 5871-4:2007 *Specification for the installation and maintenance of gas fires, convector heaters, fire/back boilers and decorative fuel effect gas appliances. Independent gas-fired flueless fires, convector heaters and heating stoves of nominal heat input not exceeding 6 kW (2nd and 3rd family gases).*

Section 3: Oil-fired space and water heating

3.1 Scope of guidance

This section provides guidance on the specification of oil-fired space heating and hot water systems[17] in dwellings to meet relevant energy efficiency requirements in the Building Regulations. The guidance applies to the following types of oil-fired heating system:

- wet central heating systems

- range cookers with integral central heating boilers

- vaporising appliances providing secondary heating or hot water

- fixed independent space heating devices.

3.2 Oil-fired wet central heating systems

New systems

New systems for oil-fired central heating in new and existing dwellings should meet the minimum standards for:

a. boiler efficiency, system circulation, hot water storage, system preparation and commissioning in Table 11

b. boiler interlock, zoning, and time and temperature control of the heating and hot water circuits in Table 12

c. pipework insulation in Table 14.

Work on existing systems

Components installed as replacements in existing systems should meet the same standards as for new systems, except where indicated otherwise in Table 13.

Table 13 in addition identifies good practice upgrades to the rest of the system when making planned and emergency replacements that go beyond the requirements of the Building Regulations.

---

17 All oil appliances must be installed by a competent person. The installation should follow the manufacturer's instructions and should comply with all relevant parts of the Building Regulations and, for wet systems, the Water Regulations.

Table 11 Recommended minimum standards for efficiency, system circulation, hot water storage, system preparation and commissioning for oil-fired wet central heating systems

	Minimum standard	Supplementary information
1.0 Efficiency	**Regular boilers** a. The boiler should be of the condensing type. b. The boiler SEDBUK 2009 efficiency should not be less than 88%. c. In existing dwellings, compliance with the requirements for boiler efficiency can be demonstrated by following the guidance in the DCLG *Guide to the condensing boiler installation assessment procedure for dwellings*. The boiler SEDBUK 2009 efficiency should not be less than 84%. **Combination boilers** d. The boiler should be of the condensing type. The boiler SEDBUK 2009 efficiency should not be less than 86%. e. In existing dwellings, compliance with the requirements for boiler efficiency can be demonstrated by following the guidance in the DCLG *Guide to the condensing boiler installation assessment procedure for dwellings*. The boiler SEDBUK 2009 efficiency should not be less than 82%. **Range cooker boilers** f. The boiler efficiency for heating boilers that are combined with range cookers should be as defined in Section 3.3 *Oil-fired cookers with integral central heating boilers*.	The Boiler Efficiency Database at www.boilers.org.uk is part of the SAP Product Characteristics Database (PCDB) and displays separate SAP winter and summer seasonal efficiencies for boilers held within it. SAP 2012 (available at www.bre.co.uk/sap2012) uses these values to calculate the carbon dioxide emission rate for a dwelling. SAP winter and summer seasonal efficiencies are derived from SEDBUK 2009 values. SEDBUK 2009 and SEDBUK 2005 efficiency values are different. If the SEDBUK efficiency in a boiler manufacturer's literature does not state whether it is SEDBUK 2009 or SEDBUK 2005, it should be assumed to be SEDBUK 2005. Minimum SEDBUK 2005 efficiency values for boilers are set out in Table 1 and in the 2010 edition of this guide. The DCLG *Guide to the condensing boiler installation assessment procedure for dwellings* sets out the approved procedure for establishing the exceptional circumstances in which boilers may be of the non-condensing type. Systems with condensing boilers should be designed to have low primary return water temperatures, preferably less than 55°C, to maximise condensing operation. Low return water temperatures can be obtained through techniques such as weather compensation and the use of low temperature heat emitters (for example correctly-sized radiators and underfloor heating elements). Low temperature heat emitters will also be compatible with low temperature heat generators, such as heat pumps, that might be installed as replacements in the future.
2.0 System circulation	a. Space heating systems and domestic hot water primary circuits should have fully pumped circulation. b. If the boiler manufacturer's instructions advise installation of a bypass, an automatic bypass valve should be provided and the manufacturer's instructions on minimum pipe length followed.	

Table 11 Recommended minimum standards for efficiency, system circulation, hot water storage, system preparation and commissioning for oil-fired wet central heating systems *(continued)*

	Minimum standard	Supplementary information

3.0
Hot water storage
	a. Vented copper hot water storage cylinders should comply with the heat loss and heat exchanger requirements of BS 1566-1:2002.
	
	b. Copper hot water storage combination units should comply with BS 3198:1981.
	
	c. Primary storage systems should meet the insulation requirements of the Hot Water Association *Performance specification for thermal stores*.
	
	d. Unvented hot water storage system products should comply with BS EN 12897:2006 or an equivalent standard.
	
	e. The standing heat loss for all hot water storage vessels in a., b., c. and d. above should not exceed $Q = 1.15 \times (0.2 + 0.051V^{2/3})$ kWh/day, where V is the volume of the cylinder in litres.
	
	f. All hot water vessels should carry a label with the following information:
	
	  i. type of vessel (vented, unvented, combination unit or thermal store)
	
	  ii. nominal capacity in litres
	
	  iii. standing heat loss in kWh/day
	
	  iv. heat exchanger performance in kW
	
	  v. reference to product compliance with relevant standard (e.g. BS 1566-1, BS EN 12897) and logos of accreditation bodies as required.
	
	For labelling requirements for other heat inputs, see relevant sections (e.g. Section 11 for solar).
		If a vented cylinder is not made from copper then the heat loss and heat exchange characteristics should be tested in accordance with BS EN 12897:2006.
		
		The HWA thermal storage specification is available from www.hotwater.org.uk.
		
		British Standards
		
		BS 1566-1:2002 *Copper indirect cylinders for domestic purposes. Open vented copper cylinders. Requirements and test methods.*
		
		BS EN 12897:2006 *Water supply. Specification for indirectly heated unvented (closed) storage water heaters.*
		
		BS 3198:1981 *Copper hot water storage combination units for domestic purposes.*

Table 11 Recommended minimum standards for efficiency, system circulation, hot water storage, system preparation and commissioning for oil-fired wet central heating systems *(continued)*

	Minimum standard	Supplementary information
4.0 System preparation and water treatment	a. Central heating systems should be thoroughly cleaned and flushed out before installing a new boiler. b. During final filling of the system, a chemical water treatment inhibitor meeting the manufacturer's specification or other appropriate standard should be added to the primary circuit to control corrosion and the formation of scale and sludge. c. Installers should also refer to the boiler manufacturer's installation instructions for appropriate treatment products and special requirements for individual boiler models. d. Where the mains total water hardness exceeds 200 parts per million, provision should be made to treat the feed water to water heaters and the hot water circuit of combination boilers to reduce the rate of accumulation of limescale. e. For solar thermal systems, see Section 11.	Inhibitors should be BuildCert approved or equivalent. Limescale can be controlled by the use of chemical limescale inhibitors, combined corrosion and limescale inhibitors, polyphosphate dosing, electrolytic scale reducers or water softeners. The relevant standard for water treatment is BS 7593:2006 *Code of practice for treatment of water in domestic hot water central heating systems.* BS 7593 notes that "naturally soft waters of low alkalinity or those supplied via a base-exchange resin softener have an increased potential for corrosion, and, if they are used in any central heating system, a corrosion inhibitor specifically formulated for the purpose should be added and properly maintained." Manufacturers should be consulted for advice, paying particular attention to dosage levels. Special radiator valves are available that will seal off the radiator as well as the heating circuit to prevent loss of inhibitor when removing a radiator for service or maintenance. A filter can also be fitted to the central heating circuit to help maintain the efficiency and reliability of the system.

Table 11 Recommended minimum standards for efficiency, system circulation, hot water storage, system preparation and commissioning for oil-fired wet central heating systems *(continued)*

	Minimum standard	Supplementary information
5.0 Commissioning	a. On completion of the installation of a boiler or a hot water storage system, together with associated equipment such as pipework, pumps and controls, the equipment should be commissioned in accordance with the manufacturer's instructions. These instructions will be specific to the particular boiler or hot water storage system. b. The installer should explain fully to the user how to operate the system in an energy efficient manner, and leave behind any user manuals provided by manufacturers.	The *Oil Controlled Document System* (as produced and managed by OFTEC) can be used to show that oil-fired appliances and related systems have been installed and commissioned satisfactorily by listing and recording works and checks which are deemed necessary for the efficient operation of the appliance and system in compliance with the Building Regulations. A copy of each completed form is left with the householder or agent for record and/or Building Control inspection purposes, and a copy is retained by the issuing installer and engineer. OFTEC branded forms are provided for the use of OFTEC Registered Competent Persons and non-OFTEC branded forms are available for others carrying out oil-fired installation and commissioning works. To assist installers OFTEC oil appliance manufacturing members may provide forms CD/10 and CD/11 with their equipment. **Controlled Document CD/10** Installing engineers should complete OFTEC Form CD/10 to show that they have completed the installation of an oil-fired appliance and controls and wet system commissioning prior to final appliance commissioning. **Controlled Document CD/11** Commissioning engineers of oil-fired appliances should complete OFTEC Form CD/11 to record and show that they have completed the commissioning of the appliance and that they have left it operating in a safe and efficient manner.

Table 12 Recommended minimum controls for oil-fired wet central heating systems[1]

Control type	Minimum standard
1.0 Boiler interlock	a. System controls should be wired so that when there is no demand for space heating or hot water, the boiler and pump are switched off.
2.0 Zoning	a. Dwellings with a total floor area > 150 m^2 should have at least two space heating zones, each with an independently controlled heating circuit[2].
	b. Dwellings with a total floor area[3] ≤ 150 m^2 may have a single space heating zone[4].
3.0 Control of space heating	a. Each space heating circuit should be provided with:
	i. independent time control, and either:
	ii. a room thermostat or programmable room thermostat located in a reference room[5] served by the heating circuit, together with individual radiator controls such as thermostatic radiator valves (TRVs) on all radiators outside the reference rooms, or
	iii. individual networked radiator controls in each room on the circuit.
4.0 Control of hot water	a. Domestic hot water circuits supplied from a hot water store (i.e. not produced instantaneously as by a combination boiler) should be provided with:
	i. independent time control, and
	ii. electric temperature control using, for example, a cylinder thermostat and a zone valve or three-port valve. (If the use of a zone valve is not appropriate, as with thermal stores, a second pump could be substituted for the zone valve.)

Notes
[1] Always also follow manufacturers' instructions.
[2] A heating circuit refers to a pipework run serving a number of radiators that is controlled by its own zone valve.
[3] The relevant floor area is the area within the insulated envelope of the dwelling, including internal cupboards and stairwells.
[4] The SAP notional dwelling assumes at least two space heating zones for all floor areas, unless the dwelling is single storey, open plan with a living area $> 70\%$ of the total floor area.
[5] A reference room is a room that will act as the main temperature control for the whole circuit and where no other form of system temperature control is present.

Table 13 Recommended minimum standards when replacing components of oil-fired wet central heating systems[1]

Component	Reason	Minimum standard	Good practice[2]
1.0 **Hot water cylinder**	Emergency	a. For copper vented cylinders and combination units, the standing losses should not exceed $Q = 1.28 \times (0.2 + 0.051V^{2/3})$ kWh/day, where V is the volume of the cylinder in litres. b. Install an electric temperature control, such as a cylinder thermostat. Where the cylinder or installation is of a type that precludes the fitting of wired controls, install either a wireless or thermo-mechanical hot water cylinder thermostat or electric temperature control. c. If separate time control for the heating circuit is not present, use of single time control for space heating and hot water is acceptable.	a. Upgrade gravity-fed systems to fully pumped. b. Install a boiler interlock and separate timing for space heating and hot water.
	Planned	d. Install a boiler interlock and separate timing for space heating and hot water.	c. Upgrade gravity-fed systems to fully pumped.
2.0 **Boiler**	Emergency/ planned	a. The efficiency of the new appliance should be as specified for new systems in Table 11 and not significantly less than the efficiency of the appliance being replaced – as set out in paragraph 1.8. b. Install a boiler interlock as defined for new systems. c. Time and temperature control should be installed for the heating system.	a. Upgrade gravity-fed systems to fully pumped. b. Fit individual radiator controls such as thermostatic radiator valves (TRVs) on all radiators except those in the reference room.
3.0 **Radiator**	Emergency		a. Fit a TRV to the replacement radiator if in a room without a room thermostat.
	Planned		b. Fit TRVs to all radiators in rooms without a room thermostat.
4.0 **New heating system – existing pipework retained**	Planned	a. Install a boiler interlock as defined for new systems. b. Fit individual radiator controls such as TRVs on all radiators except those in the reference room.	a. In dwellings with a total floor area > 150 m², install at least two heating circuits, each with independent time and temperature control, together with individual radiator controls such as TRVs on all radiators except those in the reference rooms.

Notes
[1]   Always also follow manufacturers' instructions.
[2]   Best practice would be as for a new system.

Table 14 Recommended minimum standards for insulation of pipework in oil-fired wet central heating systems

Minimum standard	Supplementary information
a. Pipes should be insulated to comply with the maximum permissible heat loss indicated in the Supplementary information column, and labelled accordingly, as follows:	(see table below)

Pipe outside diameter (mm)	Maximum heat loss (W/m)
8	7.06
10	7.23
12	7.35
15	7.89
22	9.12
28	10.07
35	11.08
42	12.19
54	14.12

Minimum standard (continued):

  i. Primary circulation pipes for heating circuits should be insulated wherever they pass outside the heated living space or through voids which communicate with and are ventilated from unheated spaces.

  ii. Primary circulation pipes for domestic hot water circuits should be insulated throughout their length, subject only to practical constraints imposed by the need to penetrate joists and other structural elements.

  iii. All pipes connected to hot water storage vessels, including the vent pipe, should be insulated for at least 1 metre from their points of connection to the cylinder (or they should be insulated up to the point where they become concealed).

  iv. If secondary circulation is used, all pipes kept hot by that circulation should be insulated.

b. Whenever a boiler or hot water storage vessel is replaced in an existing system, any pipes that are exposed as part of the work or are otherwise accessible should be insulated as recommended above – or to some lesser standard where practical constraints dictate.

Supplementary information (continued):

In assessing the thickness of insulation required, standardised conditions should be assumed in all compliance calculations, based on a horizontal pipe at 60°C in still air at 15°C.

Further guidance on converting heat loss limits to insulation thickness for specific thermal conductivities is available in TIMSA *HVAC guidance for achieving compliance with Part L of the Building Regulations*.

Insulation of pipework in unheated areas

It may be necessary to protect central heating and hot water pipework in unheated areas against freezing. Guidance is available in:

- BS 5422:2009 *Method for specifying thermal insulating materials for pipes, tanks, vessels, ductwork and equipment operating within the temperature range -40°C to +700°C.*

- BRE Report No 262 *Thermal insulation: avoiding risks, 2002 edition.*

3.3 Oil-fired range cookers with integral central heating boilers

This section provides guidance on the specification of oil-fired range cookers with integral central heating boilers for space heating and hot water in dwellings.

Note: The guidance applies only to twin-burner cooker boilers, which should not be confused with the type of range cooker described as a single burner 'dry heat' range cooker. The latter is intended only to provide a cooking function, is not included in SAP 2012 calculations, and does not come within the scope of the Building Regulations energy efficiency requirements.

Where oil-fired range cookers with an integral central heating boiler are provided as part of new systems or as replacement components in existing systems:

a. The appliance should have two independently controlled burners (one for the cooking function and one for the boiler).

b. The SEDBUK 2009 efficiency of the integral boiler should not be less than 80%.

c. The manufacturer's declaration of appliance performance and SEDBUK value should include the following words:

  i. *Seasonal efficiency (SEDBUK) = xx%*

ii.   *Case heat emission value = yy kW*

iii.   *Heat transfer to water at full load = zz kW*

iv.   *The efficiency values may be used in the UK Government's Standard Assessment Procedure (SAP) for the energy rating of dwellings. The test data from which they have been calculated has been certified by {insert name and/or identification of Notified Body}.*

If the integral boiler is a condensing boiler, the declaration should make clear whether the efficiency has been calculated in accordance with SEDBUK 2005 or SEDBUK 2009. If it does not, then SEDBUK 2005 must be assumed. See www.rangeefficiency.org.uk.

d.   The integral boiler should meet the minimum standards for oil-fired central heating systems in Tables 11, 12 and 14 for system circulation, hot water storage, system preparation, commissioning, controls and insulation.

3.4 Continuously-burning oil-fired vaporising appliances providing secondary heating or hot water

This section provides guidance on the specification of oil-fired vaporising appliances providing secondary heating or hot water for dwellings. The guidance does not apply to appliances which have been converted from another fuel (for example from solid fuel to oil).

Oil-fired vaporising appliances provided with new systems or as replacement components in existing systems should meet the minimum standards for controls in Table 15.

Table 15   Recommended minimum controls for continuously burning oil-fired vaporising appliances

Appliance type	Minimum standard	Supplementary information
a. Manually operated appliance, e.g. room heater.	The integral manual controls as provided by appliance manufacturer.	Information about the use of controls should be clearly stated in the manufacturer's literature.
b. Electrically operated (modulating) appliance, e.g. room heater.	The integral or remote thermostatic controls as provided (or specified) by the appliance manufacturer.	
Automatic on/off vaporising appliances		
c. Room heater providing (secondary) space heating.	The integral thermostatic controls as provided by the appliance manufacturer.	
d. Room heater providing domestic hot water and (secondary) space heating.	The integral or remote thermostatic controls as provided (or specified) by the appliance manufacturer.	

3.5 Oil-fired fixed independent space heating appliances

This section provides guidance on the specification of oil-fired fixed independent appliances for primary or secondary space heating in dwellings.

Oil-fired fixed independent appliances for primary heating

Where oil-fired fixed independent space heating appliances are provided as the primary heat source in new dwellings:

a. The efficiency of the appliance (gross calorific value) should not be less than 60%. The appliance manufacturer's declaration of appliance performance should include the following words:

   The net efficiency of this appliance has been measured as specified in OFS A102:2004 and the result after conversion to gross using the appropriate factor from Table E4 of SAP 2012 is [x]%. The test data has been certified by {insert name and/or identification of Notified Body}. The efficiency value may be used in the UK Government's Standard Assessment Procedure (SAP) for energy rating of dwellings.

b. Each appliance should be capable, either independently or in conjunction with room thermostats or other suitable temperature sensing devices, of controlling the temperatures independently in areas that have different heating needs (e.g. separate sleeping and living areas).

Oil-fired fixed independent appliances for secondary heating

Oil-fired fixed independent space heating appliances in new dwellings which are provided as the secondary heat source should have an efficiency (gross calorific value) of not less than 60%.

Supplementary Information

Energy Efficiency Best Practice in Housing publications:

   CE29 *Domestic heating by oil: boiler systems.*

   CE51 *Central heating system specifications (CHeSS).*

   CE54 *Whole house boiler sizing method for houses and flats.*

OFTEC Technical Books 2, 3, 4 and 5 (see www.oftec.org).

BS EN 12828:2012 *Heating systems in buildings. Design for water-based heating systems.*

BS 5410-1:1997 *Code of practice for oil firing installations up to 45 kW output capacity for space heating and hot water supply purposes.*

Section 4: Electric heating

This section provides guidance on the specification of fixed electric heating systems for dwellings to meet relevant energy efficiency requirements in the Building Regulations.

4.1 Scope of guidance

The guidance given in this section covers the following types of fixed electric heating systems:

- electric boilers serving central heating systems

- electric warm air systems

- electric panel heaters

- electric storage systems including integrated storage/direct systems.

Portable, plug-in appliances are not covered by the Building Regulations or by this guide.

4.2 Electric boilers serving central heating systems

Electric boilers serving wet central heating provided with new systems or as replacement components in existing systems should meet the minimum standards for:

a. system circulation, system preparation and commissioning in Table 16

b. boiler interlock, zoning, and time control and temperature control of heating and hot water circuits in Table 17

c. hot water storage systems in Table 18

d. pipework insulation in Table 19.

Table 16 Recommended minimum standards for system circulation, preparation and commissioning for electric wet central heating systems

	Minimum standard	Supplementary information
1.0 System circulation	a. Systems for space heating and domestic hot water primary circuits in new dwellings should have fully pumped circulation. b. If the boiler manufacturer's instructions advise installation of a bypass, then an automatic bypass valve should be used.	
2.0 System preparation and water treatment	a. Central heating systems should be thoroughly cleaned and flushed before installing a new boiler. b. During final filling of the system a chemical water treatment formulation should be added to the primary circuit to control corrosion and the formation of scale and sludge. c. Installers should also refer to the boiler manufacturer's installation instructions for appropriate treatment products and special requirements for individual boiler models. d. Where the mains total water hardness exceeds 200 parts per million, provision should be made to treat the feed water to water heaters and the hot water circuit of combination boilers to reduce the rate of accumulation of limescale.	Inhibitors should be BuildCert approved or equivalent. Limescale can be controlled by the use of chemical limescale inhibitors, combined corrosion and limescale inhibitors, polyphosphate dosing, electrolytic scale reducers or water softeners. The relevant standard for water treatment is BS 7593:2006 *Code of practice for treatment of water in domestic hot water central heating systems*. BS 7593 notes that "naturally soft waters of low alkalinity or those supplied via a base-exchange resin softener have an increased potential for corrosion, and, if they are used in any central heating system, a corrosion inhibitor specifically formulated for the purpose should be added and properly maintained." Manufacturers should be consulted for advice, paying particular attention to dosage levels. Special radiator valves are available that will seal off the radiator as well as the heating circuit to prevent loss of inhibitor when removing a radiator for service or maintenance. A filter can also be fitted to the central heating circuit to help maintain the efficiency and reliability of the system.
3.0 Commissioning	a. Manufacturers' instructions for commissioning should be followed and a commissioning record should be completed to show compliance. b. The installer should explain fully to the user how to operate the system in an energy efficient manner, and leave behind any user manuals provided by manufacturers.	

Table 17 Recommended minimum controls for electric wet central heating systems[1]

Control type	Minimum standard
1.0 Boiler temperature control	a. The boiler should be fitted with a flow temperature control and be capable of modulating the power input to the primary water depending on space heating conditions.
2.0 Boiler interlock	a. If the boiler supplies domestic hot water, system controls should be wired so that when there is no demand for space heating or hot water, the boiler and pump are switched off.
3.0 Zoning	a. Dwellings with a total floor area > 150 m² should have at least two space heating zones, each with an independently controlled heating circuit[2].
	b. Dwellings with a total floor area[3] ≤ 150 m² may have a single space heating zone[4].
4.0 Control of space heating	a. Each space heating circuit should be provided with:
	i. independent time control and either:
	ii. a room thermostat or programmable room thermostat located in a reference room[5] served by the heating circuit, together with individual radiator controls such as thermostatic radiator valves (TRVs) on all radiators outside the reference rooms, or
	iii. individual networked radiator controls in each room on the circuit.
5.0 Control of hot water	a. Domestic hot water circuits supplied from a boiler and hot water store should be provided with:
	i. independent time control, and
	ii. electric temperature control using, for example, a cylinder thermostat and a zone valve or three-port valve. (If the use of a zone valve is not appropriate, as with thermal stores, a second pump could be substituted for the zone valve.)

Notes
[1] Always also follow manufacturers' instructions.
[2] A heating circuit refers to a pipework run serving a number of radiators that is controlled by its own zone valve.
[3] The relevant floor area is the area within the insulated envelope of the dwelling, including internal cupboards and stairwells.
[4] The SAP notional dwelling assumes at least two space heating zones for all floor areas, unless the dwelling is single storey, open plan with a living area $> 70\%$ of the total floor area.
[5] A reference room is a room that will act as the main temperature control for the whole circuit and where no other form of system temperature control is present.

Supplementary information

More details on control systems can be found in manufacturers' literature and on The Association of Controls Manufacturers (TACMA) website at www.heatingcontrols.org.uk.

Controls may be provided by any boiler management control system that meets the specified zoning, timing and temperature and boiler interlock control requirements.

Table 18 Recommended minimum standards for hot water storage in electric wet central heating systems

	Minimum standard
1.0 **Vented systems, including cylinders heated primarily by electricity**	a. Vented copper hot water storage vessels should comply with BS 1566-1:2002 or BS 3198:1981. b. Vented cylinders in materials other than copper should also be labelled as complying with the heat loss requirements of BS 1566-1:2002. c. For vented replacements, electrically heated combination units should be insulated such that the heat loss does not exceed the value $Q = 1.28 \times (0.2 + 0.051V^{2/3})$ kWh/day, where V is the nominal cylinder volume in litres. This applies to electrically heated combination units as well as other electrically heated cylinders. d. In vented new systems, electrically heated combination units should be insulated such that the heat loss does not exceed the value $Q = 1.15 \times (0.2 + 0.051V^{2/3})$ kWh/day, where V is the nominal cylinder volume in litres. This applies to electrically heated combination units as well as other electrically heated cylinders.
2.0 **Unvented systems, including cylinders heated primarily by electricity**	a. Products should comply with BS EN 12897:2006 or an equivalent standard. b. Cylinders heated primarily by electricity should be insulated such that their heat loss does not exceed $Q = 1.15 \times (0.2 + 0.051V^{2/3})$ kWh/day, where V is the nominal cylinder volume in litres. This applies to electrically heated combination units as well as other electrically heated cylinders.
3.0 **Vented and unvented systems, including cylinders heated primarily by electricity**	a. Cylinders should either be factory fitted with, or have provision for, two thermostatically controlled electrical heating elements or immersion heaters. b. The lower element should be capable of heating up at least 85% of the cylinder contents. c. The upper element should be capable of heating at least 60 litres of water. d. The lower element should be connected to utilise the 'off peak' electricity tariff and the upper for boost operation. e. The vessel should be designed such that following reheating to 60°C from the off peak element, at least 80% of the contents can be drawn off at 45°C or above at a flow rate of 0.25 l/s.
4.0 **Primary stores**	a. Primary storage systems should meet the insulation requirements of the Hot Water Association *Performance specification for thermal stores*. b. Unvented hot water storage products should comply with a relevant standard as set by an accredited test body such as the British Board of Agrément, the Water Research Council or KIWA.

5.0
Labelling
	a. All hot water storage vessels should carry a label with the following information:
	
	  i. type of vessel
	
	  ii. nominal capacity in litres
	
	  iii. standing heat loss in kWh/day
	
	  iv. heat exchanger performance in kW.
	
	b. Vented copper hot water cylinders should carry clear labelling on the product such as a BSI Kitemark, registered firm status or reference to an equivalent quality control scheme.
	
	c. Vented cylinders which are not of copper construction should be labelled as complying with the heat loss and heat exchanger requirements of BS 1566-1.
	
	d. For labelling of hot water storage vessels in solar thermal systems, see Section 11.

Supplementary information

BS 1566-1:2002 *Copper indirect cylinders for domestic purposes. Open vented copper cylinders. Requirements and test methods.*

BS 3198:1981 *Specification for copper hot water storage combination units for domestic purposes.*

BS EN 12897:2006 *Water supply. Specification for indirectly heated unvented (closed) storage water heaters.*

Table 19 Recommended minimum standards for insulation of pipework in central heating systems with electric boilers

Minimum standard	Supplementary information
a. Pipes should be insulated to comply with the maximum permissible heat loss indicated in the Supplementary information column, and labelled accordingly, as follows:	(table below)

Pipe outside diameter (mm)	Maximum heat loss (W/m)
8	7.06
10	7.23
12	7.35
15	7.89
22	9.12
28	10.07
35	11.08
42	12.19
54	14.12

Minimum standard

a. Pipes should be insulated to comply with the maximum permissible heat loss indicated in the Supplementary information column, and labelled accordingly, as follows:

   i. Primary circulation pipes for heating circuits should be insulated wherever they pass outside the heated living space or through voids which communicate with and are ventilated from unheated spaces.

   ii. Primary circulation pipes for domestic hot water circuits should be insulated throughout their length, subject only to practical constraints imposed by the need to penetrate joists and other structural elements.

   iii. All pipes connected to hot water storage vessels, including the vent pipe, should be insulated for at least 1 metre from their points of connection to the cylinder (or they should be insulated up to the point where they become concealed).

   iv. If secondary circulation is used, all pipes kept hot by that circulation should be insulated.

b. Whenever a boiler or hot water storage vessel is replaced in an existing system, any pipes that are exposed as part of the work or are otherwise accessible should be insulated as recommended above – or to some lesser standard where practical constraints dictate.

Supplementary information

In assessing the thickness of insulation required, standardised conditions should be assumed in all compliance calculations, based on a horizontal pipe at 60°C in still air at 15°C.

Further guidance on converting heat loss limits to insulation thickness for specific thermal conductivities is available in TIMSA *HVAC guidance for achieving compliance with Part L of the Building Regulations.*

Insulation of pipework in unheated areas

It may be necessary to protect central heating and hot water pipework in unheated areas against freezing. Guidance is available in:

- BS 5422:2009 *Method for specifying thermal insulating materials for pipes, tanks, vessels, ductwork and equipment operating within the temperature range -40°C to +700°C.*

- BRE Report No 262 *Thermal insulation: avoiding risks,* 2002 edition.

4.3 Electric heating systems (other than electric boilers serving central heating)

This section provides guidance on the following types of fixed electric heating systems:

- electric warm air systems

- electric panel heaters

- electric storage systems including integrated storage/direct systems.

Portable, plug-in appliances are not covered by this guide.

Fixed electric heating systems (other than with electric boilers) should meet the minimum standards for time and temperature control in Table 20.

Table 20 Recommended minimum controls for primary and secondary electric heating systems (other than with electric boilers)

System	Control type	Minimum standard	Supplementary information

Warm air	**1.0**
	Time and temperature control, integral to the heater or external
		a. Systems should be provided with:
		  i. a time switch/programmer and room thermostat, or
		  ii. a programmable room thermostat.	

	2.0
	Zone control
		a. Dwellings with a total floor area $\leq$ 150 m² should have at least two space heating zones with independent temperature control, one of which is assigned to the living area.
		
		b. Dwellings with a total floor area $>$ 150 m² should have at least two space heating zones with independent temperature *and* time control. Time control may be provided using:
		  i. multiple heating zone programmers, or
		  ii. a single multi-channel programmer, or
		  iii. programmable room thermostats, or
		  iv. separate timers to each circuit, or
		  v. a combination of (iii) and (iv) above.
		
		c. In single-storey, open-plan dwellings in which the living area is greater than 70% of the total floor area, sub-zoning of temperature control is not appropriate.	

Panel heaters	**3.0** **Local time and temperature control**	a. Time control should be by a programmable time switch integrated into the appliance or by a separate time switch. b. Individual temperature control should be by integral thermostats or by separate room thermostats or programmable room thermostats.	Panel heaters provide instantaneous heat.
Storage heaters	**4.0** **Charge control**	a. Automatic control of input charge should be provided.	Charge control is the ability to detect the internal temperature and adjust the charging of the heater accordingly.
	5.0 **Temperature control**	a. Temperature control should be by adjusting the rate of heat release from the appliance, using an adjustable damper or other thermostatically-controlled method.	

Section 5: Solid fuel heating

5.1 Scope of guidance

This section provides guidance on meeting the energy efficiency standards in the Building Regulations for the following types of solid fuel heating appliances and systems used to deliver primary and secondary heating:

- batch-fed open fires

- batch-fed and automatic-feed dry room heaters/stoves

- batch-fed log and multi-fuel appliances

- automatic-feed pellet stoves with and without boilers

- batch-fed and automatic-feed room heaters with boilers

- batch-fed cookers with boilers not exceeding 7.5 kW

- batch-fed independent boilers and automatic-feed anthracite, wood pellet, wood chip and wood log fired independent boilers

- central heating systems using certain types of solid fuel appliances.

The guidance covers the following types of solid fuel: coal, anthracite, manufactured smokeless fuel, dual-fuel, wood logs, wood pellets and wood chips.

5.2 Solid fuel appliances for primary heating

Solid fuel appliances provided with new systems or as replacements in existing systems for primary heating in dwellings should have an efficiency (gross calorific value) not less than specified in Table 21 for that category of appliance.

Table 21 Solid fuel appliance categories and recommended minimum efficiencies

Category	Appliance description	Minimum efficiency (gross calorific value)	Feed
B1	Simple open fire – inset	37%	Batch
B2	Open fire – freestanding convector	47%	Batch
B3	Open fire – inset convector	45% (mineral fuels) 43% (wood fuels)	
C1/2	Open fire and boiler – inset or freestanding	50%	Batch
D1/2/3	Open fire + high output boiler – trapezium and rectangular grates	63%	Batch
D4	Open fire + high output boiler – rectangle	63%	Batch
E1	Dry room heater (dry stove)	65%	Batch/auto
E2	Dry room heater – wood logs only	65%	Batch
E3	Dry room heater – multi-fuel	65%	Batch
E4	Dry room heater – pellet stove	65% part load 70% nominal load	Auto
F	Room heater with boiler	67% (mineral fuels and wood logs) 70% (wood pellets – part load) 75% (wood pellets – nominal load)	Batch/auto
G1	Cooker without boiler not exceeding 3.5 kW	65% (mineral fuels) 55% (wood fuels)	Batch
G2	Cooker with heating boiler exceeding 3.5 kW	65% (mineral fuels) 60% (wood fuels)	Batch
J2	Independent boiler – wood logs only	75%	Batch
J3	Independent boiler – multi-fuel	65% (mineral fuels) 75% (wood logs)	Batch
J4	Independent boiler – anthracite	70% up to 20.5 kW 75% above 20.5 kW	Auto
J5	Independent boiler – wood/pellets/chips	75% nominal load 70% part load	Auto
	Slow heat release appliances	65%	Batch
	One-off tiled/mortared stoves	70%	Batch

Supplementary information

Minimum efficiencies

Minimum efficiencies for solid fuel appliances are published in the *Official guide to HETAS approved solid fuel products and services*, and on the website www.hetas.co.uk. Manufacturers' efficiency figures may be higher than those indicated and should be used where independently certified against the harmonised European Standards now in place.

Carbon emission factors

Solid fuels include wood in various forms, different types of coal, and manufactured solid fuels, and consequently there is a range of associated CO_2 emission factors. These factors are as important as appliance efficiency when selecting a boiler. CO_2 emission factors (kgCO_2/kWh) for generic types of solid fuel given in SAP 2012 Table 12 are:

House coal: traditional British coal, burns with smoky flame	0.394
Anthracite: mineral fuel with high carbon content, burns very cleanly	0.394
Manufactured smokeless fuel: mineral fuel usually made from anthracite	0.433
Wood logs: renewable wood logs either purchased or from own land	0.019
Wood pellets in bags: mechanically compressed sawdust	0.039
Bulk wood pellets: as above, delivered in bulk	0.039
Wood chips: chipped wood, processed on site	0.016
Dual-fuel: UK 'typical blend' of logs and mineral fuel as burnt on a dual-fuel stove	0.226

Smoke control

Within local authority smoke control areas, only anthracite or other authorised smokeless fuels may be used, unless the property is fitted with an exempted appliance. An exempted appliance is one that has been approved by Parliamentary Statutory Instrument for installation in smoke control areas and prospective purchasers should check that the appliance and intended fuel are permitted. A list of currently authorised fuels and exempted appliances is given on the web site www.uksmokecontrolareas.co.uk.

Outside a smoke control area, house coal or wood can be burnt on non-exempted appliances. Wood should always be seasoned to a moisture content appropriate to the design and performance of the appliance, for example not exceeding 20% in log wood, to ensure maximum performance and limit the occurrence of condensation and deposits in the chimney system.

All solid fuel appliances require appropriate soot-fire resistant chimneys discharging at high level locations as defined within the Building Regulations. Details of HETAS-approved chimney products independently tested and approved to accepted standards can be found on the HETAS website. The natural ventilation rates of these chimneys may be less than the default values listed within SAP 2012; the use of these more accurate values will reduce SAP calculated CO_2 emissions.

5.3 Central heating systems using certain types of solid fuel appliances

This section provides guidance on the following types of solid fuel appliance used to deliver primary heating as part of a central heating system:

- batch-fed open fires with high output boilers (appliance types D1 to D4 in Table 21)

- batch-fed and automatic-feed room heaters and stoves with boilers (appliance type F in Table 21)

- batch-fed cookers with boilers (appliance type G2 in Table 21)

- batch-fed independent boilers and automatic-feed anthracite, wood log, wood pellet and wood chip-fired independent boilers (appliance types J2 to J5 in Table 21).

Unless stated otherwise, the guidance applies equally to appliances that burn wood, wood pellets, house coal, manufactured smokeless fuels and anthracite.

For central heating systems with a solid fuel appliance installed as part of a new system or as a replacement component in an existing system:

a. the appliance should be from HETAS categories D, F, G and J in Table 21 and have a minimum efficiency (gross calorific value) which is not less than the value specified for its category

b. the ratio of room heat to water heat should be appropriate for the room and total property. This will require reference to installation practice guidelines and calculation of room and property heat loss. Advice on this is given in the HETAS guide and website referred to earlier

c. circulation, fuel storage, hot water storage, system preparation, water treatment and commissioning should be to the standards in Table 22

d. control of heating and hot water circuits should be to the standards in Table 23

e. pipework should be insulated to the standards in Table 24.

Supplementary information

Turn-down values (i.e. the ratio of high to low output)

Turn-down ratios are generally very good (>10:1) for automatic-feed appliances with small fire beds.

Turn-down ratios are less good with large batch-fed appliances unless the latter are used in conjunction with a hot water accumulator.

Automatic appliances are likely to require less frequent refuelling. Automatic (e.g. electric or gas) ignition is now available for certain designs and reduces energy usage at times of low demand by allowing boiler interlock.

Some boilers have both auto-ignition and fire-extinguishing features.

Link-up systems

It is possible to connect together two or more heating appliances with boilers (at least one of which can be solid fuel-fired) to maximise flexibility and efficiency. For example, an oil or gas boiler could be combined with a wood burning stove with boiler sited in the living room. This combination with wood burning appliances will reduce overall carbon emissions. Both systems should be designed to appropriate installation codes.

Table 22 Recommended minimum standards for system circulation, fuel storage, hot water storage, system preparation and commissioning for solid fuel central heating

	Minimum standard	Supplementary information
1.0 System circulation	a. Where boiler interlock is available, fully pumped circulation should be chosen. b. The manufacturer's instructions on the sizing and positioning of heat leak radiators should be followed. c. Solid fuel appliances should not be fitted to sealed heating systems with expansion vessels, except where specifically permitted by the manufacturer or where a thermal storage interface device is used.	Most solid fuel central heating systems require a heat leak radiator to dissipate heat from the smouldering fire bed. This is commonly the bathroom towel-rail and a thermosiphon system may be used for this circuit. In some cases a fully pumped system reduces efficiency and should not be used.
2.0 Fuel storage	a. Provision should be made for storage of reasonable quantities of fuel in a convenient and dry location. The size of the storage will depend upon the requirement of the house.	No minimum quantity of fuel is specified for solid mineral fuel but bunkers greater than 250 kg are preferred as below this householders are likely to pay a delivery premium.

3.0 Hot water storage	a. Vented copper hot water storage vessels should comply with the heat loss and heat exchanger requirements of BS 1566-1:2002 or BS 3198:1981.
	
	b. Vented cylinders in materials other than copper should comply with the heat loss and heat exchanger requirements of BS 1566-1.
	
	c. Unvented hot water storage system products should comply with BS EN 12897:2006 or an equivalent standard.
	
	d. Unvented systems should not be used with gravity circulation.
	
	e. Primary storage systems should meet the insulation requirements of section 4.3.1 or 4.3.2 of the Hot Water Association *Performance specification for thermal stores*.
	
	f. Combination cylinders should comply with BS 3198 and in addition have a heat loss not exceeding $1.6 \times (0.2 + 0.51V^{2/3})$ kWh/day, where V is the volume of the hot water part of the cylinder in litres.
	
	g. All hot water storage vessels should carry a label with the following information:
	  i. type of vessel
	  ii. nominal capacity in litres
	  iii. standing heat loss in kWh/day
	  iv. type of vessel
	  v. heat exchanger performance in kW.
	
	h. Vented copper hot water cylinders should carry clear labelling on the product such as a BSI Kitemark, registered firm status or reference to an equivalent quality control scheme.
		Primary hot water stores
		
		These can have a major role to play in the installation of solid fuel. The main reason for their use is to store the heat generated during slumber periods but where unvented storage cylinders are used they also provide mains pressure hot water and possible frost protection (via electric immersion heaters) for the solid fuel system. Domestic hot water outlet temperature is to be controlled at a safe level. Because of the higher than normal storage temperatures it is very important that stores are well insulated.
		
		The HWA thermal storage specification is available for free download from www.hotwater.org.uk.
		
		British Standards
		
		BS 1566-1:2002 *Copper indirect cylinders for domestic purposes. Open vented copper cylinders. Requirements and test methods.*
		
		BS 3198:1981 *Specification for copper hot water storage combination units for domestic purposes.*
		
		BS EN 12897:2006 *Water supply. Specification for indirectly heated unvented (closed) storage water heaters.*

Table 22 Recommended minimum standards for system circulation, fuel storage, hot water storage, system preparation and commissioning for solid fuel central heating *(continued)*

	Minimum standard	Supplementary information
4.0 System preparation and water treatment	a. Central heating systems should be thoroughly cleaned and flushed out before installing a new boiler. b. During final filling of the system a chemical water treatment formulation should be added to the primary circuit to control corrosion and the formation of scale and sludge. Reasonable provision would be to follow the guidance on how to prepare and commission systems given in BS 7593:2006 *Code of practice for treatment of water in domestic hot water central heating systems.* c. Installers should also refer to the boiler manufacturer's installation instructions for appropriate treatment products and special requirements for individual boiler models. d. Where the mains total water hardness exceeds 200 parts per million, provision should be made to treat the feed water to water heaters and the hot water circuit to reduce the rate of accumulation of limescale.	BS 7593 notes that "naturally soft waters of low alkalinity or those supplied via a base-exchange resin softener have an increased potential for corrosion, and, if they are used in any central heating system, a corrosion inhibitor specifically formulated for the purpose should be added and properly maintained." Manufacturers should be consulted for advice, paying particular attention to dosage levels. Special radiator valves are available that will seal off the radiator as well as the heating circuit to prevent loss of inhibitor when removing a radiator for service or maintenance. A filter can also be fitted to the central heating circuit to help maintain the efficiency and reliability of the system.
5.0 Commissioning	a. On completion of the installation of a boiler or hot water storage system, together with associated equipment such as pipework, pumps and controls, the equipment should be commissioned in accordance with the manufacturer's instructions. These instructions will be specific to the particular boiler or hot water storage system used. b. The installer should explain fully to the user how to operate the system in an energy efficient manner, and leave behind any user manuals provided by manufacturers.	Only persons who are competent should carry out the installation, e.g. installers who are registered with HETAS. Such persons will certify that they have carried out installation and commissioning in accordance with requirements in the Building Regulations and in the manufacturer's instructions (which may be more stringent). Note that the delivery of wood or coal without appropriate documentation into a smoke-control area is an offence under the Clean Air Act.

Table 23 Recommended minimum controls for solid fuel central heating systems

	Minimum standard
All appliances, except open fires	
1.0 Burning rate	a. Thermostatic control of the burning rate.
Automatic-feed appliances	
2.0 Zoning	a. Dwellings with a total floor area $\leq$ 150 m^2 should have at least two space heating zones with independent temperature control, one of which is assigned to the living area.
	b. Dwellings with a total floor area $>$ 150 m^2 should have at least two space heating zones with independent temperature and time control.
	c. For single-storey, open-plan dwellings in which the living area is greater than 70% of the total floor area, sub-zoning of temperature control is not appropriate.
3.0 Time control of space and water heating	a. Time control of space and water heating should be provided by: i. a full programmer with separate timing to each circuit, or ii. two or more separate timers providing timing control to each circuit, or iii. programmable room thermostats to the heating circuits, with separate timing of the hot water circuit.
4.0 Temperature control of space heating	a. Separate temperature control of zones within the dwelling should be provided using: i. room thermostats or programmable room thermostats in all zones, or ii. a room thermostat or programmable room thermostat in the main zone, and individual radiator controls such as thermostatic radiator valves (TRVs), or iii. a combination of (i) and (ii) above.
5.0 Temperature control of domestic hot water	a. A cylinder thermostat and a zone valve or three-port valve should be fitted to control the temperature of stored hot water. b. Non-electric hot water controllers should not be used. c. Where permitted by the manufacturer, the cylinder thermostat should be wired to provide a boiler interlock.

Supplementary information

Boiler interlock, provided by a wiring arrangement to prevent the system from operating when there is no demand for heat, should only be fitted if recommended by the manufacturer.

In some simple batch-fed or automatic appliances (without heat stores or without automatic ignition), it is not possible to switch off the heat output completely, but the appliance output can be lowered to a minimum to reduce fuel consumption.

In most solid fuel systems the room thermostat will switch off the pump, which in turn will cause the boiler to operate at minimum output.

Some automatic solid fuel systems can be fitted with weather compensation, and incorporate multi-zone control. It is important to seek guidance from the manufacturer, especially if the heating package is to include other fuels.

Controls may be provided by any boiler management control system that meets the specified zoning, timing and temperature, and boiler interlock control requirements.

The level of sophistication should generally be appropriate to and compatible with the appliance. The highest levels are only appropriate to appliances with automatic ignition.

As far as it is practicable and economic to do so when working on existing systems, controls should be upgraded to the levels defined for new systems.

Table 24 Recommended minimum standards for insulation of pipework in solid fuel central heating systems

Minimum standard	Supplementary information

Minimum standard

a. Pipes should be insulated to comply with the maximum permissible heat loss indicated in the Supplementary information column, and labelled accordingly, as follows:

  i. Primary circulation pipes for heating circuits should be insulated wherever they pass outside the heated living space or through voids which communicate with and are ventilated from unheated spaces.

  ii. Primary circulation pipes for domestic hot water circuits should be insulated throughout their length, subject only to practical constraints imposed by the need to penetrate joists and other structural elements.

  iii. All pipes connected to hot water storage vessels, including the vent pipe, should be insulated for at least 1 metre from their points of connection to the cylinder (or they should be insulated up to the point where they become concealed).

  iv. If secondary circulation is used, all pipes kept hot by that circulation should be insulated.

b. Whenever a boiler or hot water storage vessel is replaced in an existing system, any pipes that are exposed as part of the work or are otherwise accessible should be insulated as recommended above – or to some lesser standard where practical constraints dictate.

Supplementary information

Pipe outside diameter (mm)	Maximum heat loss (W/m)
8	7.06
10	7.23
12	7.35
15	7.89
22	9.12
28	10.07
35	11.08
42	12.19
54	14.12

In assessing the thickness of insulation required, standardised conditions should be assumed in all compliance calculations, based on a horizontal pipe at 60°C in still air at 15°C.

Further guidance on converting heat loss limits to insulation thickness for specific thermal conductivities is available in TIMSA *HVAC guidance for achieving compliance with Part L of the Building Regulations.*

Insulation of pipework in unheated areas

It may be necessary to protect central heating and hot water pipework in unheated areas against freezing. Guidance is available in:

- BS 5422:2009 *Method for specifying thermal insulating materials for pipes, tanks, vessels, ductwork and equipment operating within the temperature range -40°C to +700°C.*

- BRE Report No 262 *Thermal insulation: avoiding risks,* 2002 edition.

5.4 Solid fuel appliances for secondary heating

Solid fuel appliances in new and existing dwellings that provide secondary heating and are not part of a central heating system should have the minimum efficiency (gross calorific value) specified in Table 21 for the category of appliance.

Supplementary information

Minimum efficiencies

Minimum efficiencies for solid fuel appliances are published in the *Official guide to HETAS approved solid fuel products and services*, and on the website www.hetas.co.uk. Manufacturers' figures may be higher but should be used only where independently certified against the harmonised European Standards now in place.

Appliance types

The types of appliance most suitable for providing secondary heating are:

- *Open-fire with high output boiler, when used with 'link-up'*

- *Small solid fuel room heaters (stoves), especially wood-fired.*

These can be a dedicated wood burner or burn logs in a multi-fuel appliance or use pellets. They can be matched with a main heating system fired by the same or a different primary fuel or off-peak electricity to reduce carbon emissions, especially wood-fired, with or without thermostatic control. Many designs can provide heating during power cuts. Mineral fuel appliances can be chosen but the attention of designers is drawn to the probable need to supply additional measures, as the carbon emission values of these tend to be high. Mineral fuel appliances may often have slightly higher efficiencies than their wood burning counterparts. Multi-fuel room heaters can enable the user to burn renewable wood as well as an alternative to mineral fuels outside smoke control areas.

- *Small solid fuel stoves with boilers*

The efficiency of these can be higher than that of dry appliances. They can be integrated with the primary wet heating system. Multi-fuel appliances enable the householder to burn renewable wood outside smoke control areas.

- *Range cookers*

Typically appliances which are installed in a 'living area' and are designed to provide some useful heat from their case into the space in which they are located. They are available in a variety of shapes and sizes and can incorporate a boiler which can be connected to dual-fuel integrated systems (e.g. link-up). Multi-fuel versions are also available.

- *Open fires (HETAS categories B1, B2 and B3)*

Where requested, these can be fitted. They do not have thermostatic control of the burning rate and so have lower efficiencies, but they are able to burn wood logs with correspondingly low net carbon emissions. It must be stressed that large open fires with a large free face area (opening width times opening height) usually have a need for ventilation well in excess of that available in a property built to modern standards of air tightness. This is likely to lead to severe operational problems unless special steps are taken to provide the required air supply. The use of such large (simple) open fires is penalised in the SAP calculations.

Controls

Wherever possible, solid fuel appliances should have thermostatic control. (These are usually integral to appliances in categories E, F and G.) Controls should be appropriate to the level of sophistication of the appliance; automatic appliances can benefit from advanced controls.

Provision of fuel storage

The quantity of fuel consumed by secondary heating appliances is likely to be less than 1 tonne per year. However it should be stored in a dry and convenient location.

Smoke control areas

The location of the appliance within or without a smoke control area is critical to the process of optimising the choice of appliance and fuel.

For further information on solid fuel appliances, see CE47 Energy Efficiency Best Practice in Housing – *Domestic heating by solid fuel: Boiler systems*.

Standards

BS EN 12809:2001+A1:2004+AC:2006/2007 *Residential independent boilers fired by solid fuel. Nominal output up to 50 kW. Requirements and test methods.*

BS EN 12815:2001+A1:2004/2006/2007 *Residential cookers fired by solid fuel. Requirements and test methods.*

BS EN 13229:2001+A1:2003+A2:2004+AC:2006/2007 *Inset appliances including open fires fired by solid fuel. Requirements and test methods.*

BS EN 13240:2001+A2:2004+AC2006/2007 *Room heaters fired by solid fuel. Requirements and test methods.*

BS EN 15250:2007 *Slow heat release appliances fired by solid fuel. Requirements and test methods.*

BS EN 15544:2009 *One-off tiled/mortared stoves. Calculation method.*

BS EN 14785:2006 *Residential space heating appliances fired by wood pellets.*

Section 6: Community heating

6.1 Scope of guidance

This section provides guidance on the specification of community heating systems for dwellings to meet relevant energy efficiency requirements in the Building Regulations.

A community heating system is one that supplies heat to a number of dwellings from a common heat source. A system may heat a small block of flats or a large number of buildings.

The guidance in this section applies to systems that:

- supply 15 or more dwellings from a central boiler, or from a low carbon source such as combined heat and power (CHP), biofuels, heat pumps and solar panels

- distribute heat from the central source using a wet radiator system (although warm air heating and underfloor heating systems may also be used).

Metering requirements for community heating schemes are being introduced, starting in June 2014, as a result of the EU Energy Efficiency Directive. See the DECC website for details of the requirements and the technical standards that apply (for example on meter specifications): https://www.gov.uk/decc.

6.2 New and existing community heating schemes

The central heat source should comply with the requirements in the *Non-Domestic Building Services Compliance Guide* except where specified in this section.

Guidance is provided for two scenarios:

- connecting dwellings to a new community heating scheme

- connecting dwellings to an existing community heating scheme.

Connecting dwellings to a new community heating scheme

New community heating systems for both new and existing dwellings should meet the minimum standards for:

a. energy efficiency in Table 25

b. low carbon heat sources in Table 26

c. system control in Table 27

d. hot water production, storage and treatment, heat metering and commissioning in Table 28

e. insulation of pipework in Table 29 and Table 30.

Connecting dwellings to an existing community heating scheme

Where existing community heating systems are connected to new or existing dwellings:

a. If the existing community heating system is in need of replacement or improvement, a study should be carried out to assess the economic and environmental benefits of a range of options, including the use of CHP and other low carbon heat sources, especially where individual heating systems are being considered as an alternative to continuing with the community heating system.

b.   Replacement boilers should meet the minimum standards for boiler efficiency in the *Non-Domestic Building Services Compliance Guide* (available from www.planningportal.gov.uk/approveddocuments/PartL › Associated documents).

c.   If thermal energy is purchased from an existing district or community heating system, an assessment of the carbon intensity of the scheme should be carried out. Emission factors should be determined based on the particular details of the scheme, but should take account of the annual average performance of the whole system – that is, of the distribution circuits and all the heat generating plant, including any CHP, and any waste heat recovery or heat dumping. The calculation of the dwelling carbon dioxide emission rate should be carried out by a suitably qualified person, who should explain how the emission factors were derived.

d.   Controls should meet the minimum standards in Table 27.

e.   Pipework insulation should meet the minimum standards in Table 29 and Table 30.

Table 25 Recommended minimum standards for the design of community heating systems to maximise efficiency of heat generation and minimise energy use by pumps

	Minimum standard	Supplementary information
1.0 Boilers	a. Boiler-only community heating systems for new dwellings may be used provided that the target carbon dioxide emission rate (TER) for the dwelling is not exceeded. b. Boilers should be selected to comply with the boiler efficiency requirements of the *Non-Domestic Building Services Compliance Guide*.	When calculating the carbon dioxide emission rate, the type and quantity of fuel used and also the electricity needed to operate the central plant and pumps should be taken into account. For systems using condensing boilers: • To achieve high boiler efficiency, return temperatures from radiator circuits should be below 50°C. • Where instantaneous plate heat exchangers are used to produce hot water in individual dwellings the return temperature selected should be less than 40°C. • Where hot water cylinders are used the coil size should be such as to require a flow rate that results in a nominal return temperature of less than 40°C while meeting the required heat-up time. • Where hot water is produced centrally (e.g. in each block of dwellings) return temperatures should be below 40°C.
2.0 Controlling the sequencing and firing of boilers	a. Controls for boilers should follow the guidance in the *Non-Domestic Building Services Compliance Guide*, but without optimum start.	Setting occupation times is not generally possible for a group of dwellings and so optimum start controls are not a recommendation.
3.0 Minimising energy use by pumps	a. For new community heating systems, the design temperature difference for the community heating primary circuit should be greater than 20°C. b. Variable volume control systems should be used to reduce the volume of water and the pressure difference required from the pumps under part load.	Pumping energy can be minimised by optimising operating temperatures and pipe sizes to reduce installed pump power. To take full advantage of variable volume systems, variable speed pumps should be installed and controlled to deliver the required pressure difference to suit the load. Further guidance is provided in BSRIA Application Guide AG 16/2002 – *Variable-flow water systems: design, installation and commissioning guidance*.

Table 26 Recommended minimum standards for design of low carbon heat sources where these are included in community heating systems

	Minimum standard	Supplementary information
1.0 **Low carbon heat sources**	a. No minimum standard, but see Supplementary information.	Community heating systems can be designed to use low carbon heat sources to meet all or part of the heat demand, which may enable some relaxation of the U-values that would otherwise be required.
2.0 **Biofuels**	a. No minimum standard, but see Supplementary information.	Biofuels can be used to provide heat from boiler systems or as a fuel for CHP systems. Consideration should be given to operation and maintenance of the plant to ensure a long life and to prevent a later replacement by a conventional fuel system. Where a biofuel boiler is to be used in conjunction with conventionally fuelled heating boilers or electric heating, a reasonable minimum proportion of the annual heat supply from biofuels would be 45% of the annual heat demand (space, domestic hot water and process heating).
3.0 **Combined heat and power (CHP)**	a. Where CHP is used in conjunction with boiler plant, the control system should ensure that, as far as is practicable, the CHP plant operates as the lead heat source.	CHP capacity should be optimised to meet the required economic and environmental objectives. A reasonable minimum proportion of the annual heat supply from CHP would be 45% of the annual heat demand (space and domestic hot water heating). To maximise the use of CHP heat over the year, consideration should be given to the use of thermal storage to meet peaks, especially in the early morning period. The procedure given in SAP 2012 should be used to calculate the carbon dioxide emissions from CHP systems.
4.0 **Heat pumps**	a. No minimum standard, but see Supplementary information.	Heat pumps can be used as a heat source for community heating systems. Selection of operating temperatures to optimise the efficiency of the community heating system and achieve high COPs is important if carbon dioxide emissions are to be reduced. This may involve the use of underfloor heating and the provision of domestic hot water by other means. Where heat pumps are installed in conjunction with heating boilers, a reasonable minimum proportion of the annual heat supply from the heat pump would be 45% of the annual space heating demand.
5.0 **Solar**	a. No minimum standard, but see Supplementary information.	Solar thermal panels can be used as the heat source for a centralised domestic hot water system.

Table 27 Recommended minimum controls for community heating systems within dwellings

Control type	Minimum standard	Supplementary information
1.0 Zoning	a. Dwellings with a total floor area ≤ 150 m² should have at least two space heating zones with independent temperature control, one of which is assigned to the living area. b. Dwellings with a total floor area > 150 m² should have at least two space heating zones with independent temperature *and* time control.	In single-storey, open-plan dwellings in which the living area is greater than 70% of the total floor area, sub-zoning of temperature control is not appropriate.
2.0 Time control of space heating	a. Time control of space heating may be provided by: 　i.　a full programmer, or 　ii.　two or more separate timers providing timing control to each zone, or 　iii.　programmable room thermostats to the heating circuits. b. For dwellings with a total floor area > 150 m², time control for the separate space heating zones can be provided using: 　i.　multiple heating zone programmers, or 　ii.　a single multi-channel programmer.	Where the hot water is produced instantaneously, such as with a plate heat exchanger, time control is only required for space heating zones. Time control of domestic hot water heating using a cylinder is not considered essential for community heating and could be a disadvantage with CHP-based systems, increasing the morning peak demand and hence causing more use of the boiler than necessary.
3.0 Temperature control of space heating	a. Separate temperature control of zones within the dwelling should be provided using: 　i.　room thermostats or programmable room thermostats in all zones, or 　ii.　a room thermostat or programmable room thermostat in the main zone, and individual radiator controls such as thermostatic radiator valves (TRVs) on all radiators in the other zones, or 　iii.　a combination of (i) and (ii) above.	Control valves and TRVs should be two-port type to reduce flow rates under part load. Differential pressures across control valves and TRVs should be limited to ensure that the control valves work effectively and maintain shut-off.
4.0 Temperature control of domestic hot water	a. Temperature control of the domestic hot water service should be provided using two-port control valves, either electrically operated or direct-acting.	Where instantaneous heat exchangers are used the control valve should be selected to maintain steady temperatures (< ± 5°C) for a range of draw-off rates and primary differential pressures. To reduce the incidence of scaling, the control valve should shut off the primary flow when there is no domestic hot water draw off. A small intermittent flow is an advantage to maintain the temperature within the heat exchanger so as to provide more rapid heat up.
5.0 Limitation of maximum flow rate into building or dwelling	a. The maximum design flow rate into the dwelling heating system should be limited by suitable control and balancing valves to maintain the overall balance in the network and to avoid excessive pumping energy.	

Table 28 Recommended minimum standards for domestic hot water (DHW) production, storage and water treatment, heat meters and commissioning for community heating

	Minimum standard	Supplementary information
1.0 DHW production and storage	a. The hot water system should be controlled using variable volume control principles and be designed to maintain low return temperatures in the primary community heating circuit.	Hot water can be produced in four ways in community heating systems: • in individual dwellings using indirect storage cylinders • in individual dwellings using instantaneous plate heat exchangers • centrally using storage calorifiers with either an indirect coil or an external plate heat exchanger • centrally using an instantaneous plate heat exchanger. In selecting the system, consideration should be given to: • the impact on return temperatures in the community heating system • the impact on flow rates in the community heating system • the impact on heat demand profiles and compatibility with the heat source • standing losses from storage cylinders/calorifiers and the impact on energy use • the quality of service provided in terms of flow rate and temperature control • the advantages of having local storage in terms of security of supply. Where the network is extensive and hot water production is centralised, a two-stage water heating system can be used to deliver low return temperatures. In this design the return water from the space heating circuit is used to pre-heat the cold feed to the domestic hot water.
2.0 Water treatment	a. A suitable system for introduction of water treatment chemicals into the community heating system in a controlled manner with facility for monitoring of water quality should be provided.	A suitable long-term programme of water treatment is essential to preserve the life of the community heating system by limiting internal corrosion. Additional chemical and physical treatment should be evaluated especially for larger systems, including: • removal of oxygen by physical means • softened water supply • side-stream filtration • biocide.
3.0 Heat meters	a. Provision should be made in the design for including heat meters either at the time of installation or at a later date without major pipework changes.	The Energy Efficiency Directive will set stronger requirements. For up-to-date information, see https://www.gov.uk/decc

Table 28 Recommended minimum standards for domestic hot water (DHW) production, storage and water treatment, heat meters and commissioning for community heating *(continued)*

	Minimum standard	Supplementary information
4.0 Commissioning	a. The community heating system should be commissioned so that the design volume flow rates are supplied to each dwelling and there is no excessive bypassing of water that would lead to higher pumping energy use.	Where the central heat source includes a low carbon heat source, the control system should be proven by demonstrating that the low carbon heat source will normally act as the lead heat source.
	b. The flow rates in individual heat emitters should be balanced using appropriate return temperatures or by using calibrated control valves.	
	c. The systems within the dwellings should be demonstrated to the resident and suitable information provided on the operation of the controls.	

Table 29 Recommended minimum standards for insulation of internal pipework in community heating systems

Minimum standard

a. Pipes should be insulated to comply with the maximum permissible heat loss indicated in the Supplementary information column, and labelled accordingly, as follows:

  i. Primary circulation pipes for heating circuits should be insulated wherever they pass outside the heated living space or through voids which communicate with and are ventilated from unheated spaces.

  ii. Primary circulation pipes for domestic hot water circuits should be insulated throughout their length, subject only to practical constraints imposed by the need to penetrate joists and other structural elements.

  iii. All pipes connected to hot water storage vessels, including the vent pipe, should be insulated for at least 1 metre from their points of connection to the cylinder (or they should be insulated up to the point where they become concealed).

  iv. If secondary circulation is used, all pipes kept hot by that circulation should be insulated.

b. Whenever a boiler or hot water storage vessel is replaced in an existing system, any pipes that are exposed as part of the work or are otherwise accessible should be insulated as recommended above – or to some lesser standard where practical constraints dictate.

Supplementary information

Pipe outside diameter (mm)	Maximum heat loss (W/m)
8	7.06
10	7.23
12	7.35
15	7.89
22	9.12
28	10.07
35	11.08
42	12.19
54	14.12

In assessing the thickness of insulation required, standardised conditions should be assumed in all compliance calculations, based on a horizontal pipe at 60°C in still air at 15°C.

Further guidance on converting heat loss limits to insulation thickness for specific thermal conductivities is available in TIMSA *HVAC guidance for achieving compliance with Part L of the Building Regulations.*

Insulation of pipework in unheated areas

It may be necessary to protect central heating and hot water pipework in unheated areas against freezing. Guidance is available in:

* BS 5422:2009 *Method for specifying thermal insulating materials for pipes, tanks, vessels, ductwork and equipment operating within the temperature range -40°C to +700°C.*

* BRE Report No 262 *Thermal insulation: avoiding risks, 2002 edition.*

Table 30 Recommended minimum standards for insulation of external pipework in community heating systems

Minimum standard	Supplementary information
a. Community heating pipework should be insulated to the standards defined in BS EN 253 for pre-insulated pipes or to an equivalent performance for conventionally insulated pipes.	Community heating pipework typically uses pre-insulated buried pipe systems. Minimum insulation thicknesses are defined in European standards. Where pipework is run above ground the pipe insulation performance should be at least as high as that used in the buried part of the system. Enhanced insulation standards should be evaluated where community heating is supplied only from fossil-fuelled boilers or where flow temperatures over 100°C are being used. **Designing for minimum heat losses** Heat losses can be reduced by optimising operating temperatures in conjunction with the need to minimise pumping energy. Variable volume control systems will assist in maintaining low return temperatures. While some bypasses may be needed to maintain the system in a hot condition ready to meet the demand, these should be controlled to the minimum flow needed. The use of temperature controlled bypass valves where the bypass only operates when flow temperature has dropped below a set level is recommended. All pipework should be insulated to prevent uncontrolled heat loss when passing through communal spaces that may otherwise suffer from overheating.

Supplementary information

Good Practice Guide GPG 234 *Guide to community heating and CHP – Commercial, public and domestic applications.* Available from the Carbon Trust.

BS EN 13941:2009+A1:2010 *Design and installation of pre-insulated bonded pipe systems for direct heating.*

BS EN 14419:2009 *District heating pipes. Pre-insulated bonded pipe systems for directly buried hot water networks. Surveillance systems.*

BS EN 253:2009+A1:2013 *District heating pipes. Pre-insulated bonded pipe systems for directly buried hot water networks. Pipe assembly of steel service pipe, polyurethane thermal insulation and outer casing of polyethylene.*

BS EN 448:2009 *District heating pipes. Pre-insulated bonded pipe systems for directly buried hot water networks. Fitting assemblies of steel service pipes, polyurethane thermal insulation and outer casing of polyethylene.*

BS EN 488:2011 *District heating pipes. Pre-insulated bonded pipe systems for directly buried hot water networks. Steel valve assembly for steel service pipes, polyurethane thermal insulation and outer casing of polyethylene.*

BS EN 489:2009 *District heating pipes. Pre-insulated bonded pipe systems for directly buried hot water networks. Joint assembly for steel service pipes, polyurethane thermal insulation and outer casing of polyethylene.*

Section 7: Underfloor heating

7.1 Scope of guidance

This section provides guidance on the specification of underfloor heating systems in new dwellings to meet relevant energy efficiency requirements in the Building Regulations.

The guidance covers the use of hot water pipes or electric heating elements as the underfloor heat source.

7.2 Underfloor heating in new dwellings

Underfloor heating in new dwellings should meet the minimum standards for:

a. system control and safe operating temperatures in Table 31

b. floor insulation and system design to minimise distribution losses in Table 32

c. in the case of electric underfloor heating systems in new dwellings, construction and controls in Table 33.

Table 31 Recommended minimum standards for control of wet and electric underfloor heating systems

	Minimum standard	Supplementary information

1.0 System temperature control: wet and electric underfloor heating systems	a. All floor heating systems, whether warm water or electric, should be fitted with controls to ensure safe and comfortable operating temperatures.
	
	b. To prevent damage to floors and occupant discomfort, the temperature of the flow water from warm water systems connected to a high temperature (>60°C) heat source should be controlled using:
	
	  i. multi-port mixing valves and thermo-mechanical or thermo-electric actuators
	
	  ii. a separate high-limit thermostat.
	
	c. Electric floor heating systems should comply with the rules in BS 7671:2008+A1:2011 *Requirements for electrical installations*, Section 753, *Floor and ceiling heating systems*, for protection against electric shock and thermal effects, and for selection and installation of equipment.
		Mixed systems with radiators and underfloor heating connected to a common high temperature heat source may benefit from being operated at the same low water temperature.
		
		For optimum long-term efficiency, consider using weather compensating controllers with thermo-electric mixing valves.

2.0 Room temperature control: wet and electric underfloor heating systems	a. Each room should have its own thermostat, sensor or programmable thermostat. b. Where two adjacent rooms have a similar function – for example a kitchen and a utility room – it may be appropriate for both rooms to share a single temperature control.	
3.0 Time control: wet and electric underfloor heating systems	a. Dwellings with a total floor area up to 150 m² should have at least two space heating zones with independent temperature control, one of which is assigned to the living area. b. Dwellings with a total floor area >150 m² should have at least two space heating zones with independent on/off time and temperature control. c. For single-storey, open-plan dwellings in which the living area is greater than 70% of the total floor area, sub-zoning of temperature control is not appropriate. d. Thick screed floor heating systems (>65 mm) should have facilities for automatic setback of room temperature to a lower level at night or during unoccupied periods.	Facilities for automatic setback of room temperature to a lower level at night or during unoccupied periods are recommended for both electric and warm water systems.
4.0 Boiler control: wet underfloor heating systems only	a. The heating system controls should be connected so that when there is no demand for heat, the heat source and pump are switched off.	

Table 32 Recommended minimum standards for floor insulation and minimising distribution losses in wet and electric underfloor heating systems

	Minimum standard	Supplementary information
1.0 Exposed ground floors	a. Ground floors on earth, or suspended floors in contact with outside air, should be insulated to limit downward heat loss, due to the thermal resistance of the applied floor finish, to not more than 10 W/m². b. When heat output is not known but the floor finish is specified, the amount of system thermal insulation needed may be calculated based on the sum of the thermal resistance of the floor finish and the underlying heated layer, multiplied by 10. c. Floor heating systems intended for cyclical operation or installed over unheated rooms should be separated from the structural floor by a layer of thermal insulation with a thermal resistance of at least 1.25 (m²·K)/W.	
2.0 Intermediate floors with heated rooms below: wet systems	a. The intermediate floor should have a separating layer of system thermal insulation with thermal resistance as in 1.0 b above, or not less than 0.75 (m²·K)/W as specified in BS EN 1264-4.	Party floors of apartments with underfloor heating are directly coupled to the heating elements, so thermal insulation is important. In high-rise apartments, resistance values may need to exceed those specified.
3.0 Intermediate floors with heated rooms below: electric systems	a. The intermediate floor should have a separating layer of system thermal insulation with thermal resistance as in 1.0 b above, or not less than 0.5 (m²·K)/W.	
4.0 System design to minimise distribution losses	a. Underfloor heating distribution boards or warm water distribution manifolds should be located centrally between the rooms being heated, thus minimising the length of interconnecting services. b. Service pipes carrying hot water to more distant rooms should be insulated or routed through conduits to reduce distribution losses and the risk of overheating the room or floor finish.	
5.0 System commissioning and corrosion protection **Control of oxidation, biofilm, scale and sludge in warm water heating systems**	a. Commissioning warm water floor heating systems should be carried out in accordance with BS EN 1264-4. Even where plastic tubes contain oxygen gas barriers, the control of corrosion in mixed product heating systems must be addressed carefully. b. After testing and flushing with clean water, the system circulating fluid should be treated with a suitable corrosion inhibitor approved by the tube manufacturer and complying with BS 7593:2006 or DIN 4726 (2008-2010), and applied strictly in accordance with the additive manufacturer's instructions.	**Standards** BS EN 1264-4:2009 *Water based surface embedded heating and cooling systems. Installation.* BS 7593:2006 *Code of practice for treatment of water in domestic hot water central heating systems.* DIN 4726 (2008-2010) *Warm water surface heating systems and radiator connecting systems. Plastic piping systems and multi layer piping systems.* Inhibitors should be BuildCert approved or equivalent.

Table 33 Recommended minimum standards for construction and control of electric underfloor heating systems

		Minimum standard
Electric storage systems with individual room or programmable thermostats and low tariff anticipatory controls	**1.0 Construction**	a. Electric cable underfloor heating low tariff night energy storage systems should have a 65 mm minimum thickness screed for correct operation. b. Principal rooms containing 80% floor area should be assigned to low tariff heating cables and 20% of the floor area should be assigned to either direct-acting perimeter heating cables or systems such as ceiling or panel heaters in order to maximise energy efficiency.
		Supplementary information Other areas should be assigned as low tariff heating cables only (subject to heat requirements). Bathrooms and separate kitchens may have direct-acting heating cables (subject to heat requirements).
	2.0 Controls	a. Anticipatory controllers should be installed controlling low tariff input charge with external temperature sensing and floor temperature sensing. b. Programmable room thermostats with an override feature should be provided for all direct-acting zones of the system with air and floor temperature sensing capabilities to be used individually or combined.
		Supplementary information Anticipatory controllers (i.e. weather compensators) reduce night energy storage as a function of external temperature.
Electric cable, direct-acting (non-storage) systems with individual room timer or thermostat control in screeded floors	**3.0 Construction**	a. Direct-acting electric underfloor heating cables should be installed within screeds of thickness not exceeding 60 mm. b. All heated floors should be insulated in accordance with Table 32.
	4.0 Controls	a. Programmable room thermostats with a manual override feature for all heating zones with air or floor temperature sensing capabilities should be used individually or combined.
Electric cable, direct-acting systems with individual room timer or thermostat control in timber floors	**5.0 Construction**	a. Direct-acting electric underfloor heating cables installed below floor boards in voids between floor joists should be insulated in accordance with Table 32.
	6.0 Controls	a. Programmable room thermostats with a manual override feature should be provided to control space temperature and limit floor void temperature for safety and comfort in each area.
Under-tile electric floor heating systems	**7.0 Construction**	a. Direct-acting electric underfloor heating cables should be provided with a pre-fabricated mattress, or equivalent IEC 60800:2009 approved heating cable product, of thickness less than 4 mm encapsulated in tile bedding adhesive or mortar, below a ceramic or other equivalent floor finish on a thermally resistive insulation layer as in Table 32 1.0 b.
	8.0 Controls	a. Programmable room thermostats with a manual override feature should be provided to control space temperature and limit floor temperature for safety and comfort in each area.

Table 35 Heat pump technologies

Heat pump type	Warm water and hot water systems	Warm air systems
Ground source heat pump (GSHP) systems	Ground-to-water	Ground-to-air
Heat energy is extracted from the ground using closed pipe loops buried horizontally in trenches or in vertical boreholes that are connected back to the GSHP. The fluid circulating in the closed loop is normally a water/propylene glycol antifreeze mixture or accepted equivalent but some direct expansion GSHPs use refrigerant. Open loops may also be used to collect water from an aquifer and discharge via a separate aquifer downstream of the water table flow; systems of this type normally require permits from the Environment Agency. Heat extracted from the ground may be supplied to a dwelling either by a water-based heating system (ground-to-water heat pump) or by an air distribution system (ground-to-air heat pump).		
Water source heat pump (WSHP) systems	Water-to-water	Water-to-air
Heat energy is extracted indirectly from a water source using closed pipe loops as a heat exchanger. The closed loop is connected back to the water-to-water heat pump. The water source may be a lake, pond or river or other stable water source. The fluid circulating in the closed loop will normally be water but a water/propylene glycol or accepted equivalent antifreeze mixture may be used, depending on operating temperatures. Open loops may also be used subject to the permits being obtained from the Environment Agency. Heat may be supplied to the dwelling either by a water-based heating system (water-to-water heat pump) or by an air distribution system (water-to-air heat pump).		
Air source heat pump (ASHP) systems	Air-to-water	Air-to-air
Air source heat pumps extract heat directly from the ambient air. Heat is supplied to the dwelling either by a water-based heating system (air-to-water heat pump) or by an air distribution system (air-to-air heat pump). Air source heat pumps may be single package or split systems.		

Supplementary information

All heat pump systems are at their most efficient when the source temperature is as high as possible, the heat distribution temperature is as low as possible and pressure losses in air and water systems are kept to a minimum. If installed in a new dwelling, heat pumps should use refrigerants complying with the provisions of EC Regulation No 2037/2000. Heat pumps should be CE marked in accordance with applicable EU directives: e.g. the machinery safety, low voltage, pressure equipment and electromagnetic compatibility directives. If summer cooling is provided by the heat pump, it is recommended that condensate drainage from the indoor units is provided.

Section 9: Heat pumps

9.1 Scope of guidance

This section provides guidance on the specification of heat pump systems in dwellings for the provision of space heating and domestic hot water to meet relevant energy efficiency requirements in the Building Regulations.

A heat pump is a device which takes heat energy from a low temperature source and upgrades it to a higher temperature at which it can be usefully employed for heating or hot water. Heat pumps may supply all or part of the heating load.

The guidance in this section applies to the types of electrically-driven heat pump in Table 35 used as the heat generator in underfloor, warm air and medium temperature radiator heating systems, etc.

Table 35 Heat pump technologies

Heat pump type	Warm water and hot water systems	Warm air systems
Ground source heat pump (GSHP) systems	Ground-to-water	Ground-to-air
Heat energy is extracted from the ground using closed pipe loops buried horizontally in trenches or in vertical boreholes that are connected back to the GSHP. The fluid circulating in the closed loop is normally a water/propylene glycol antifreeze mixture or accepted equivalent but some direct expansion GSHPs use refrigerant. Open loops may also be used to collect water from an aquifer and discharge via a separate aquifer downstream of the water table flow; systems of this type normally require permits from the Environment Agency. Heat extracted from the ground may be supplied to a dwelling either by a water-based heating system (ground-to-water heat pump) or by an air distribution system (ground-to-air heat pump).		
Water source heat pump (WSHP) systems	Water-to-water	Water-to-air
Heat energy is extracted indirectly from a water source using closed pipe loops as a heat exchanger. The closed loop is connected back to the water-to-water heat pump. The water source may be a lake, pond or river or other stable water source. The fluid circulating in the closed loop will normally be water but a water/propylene glycol or accepted equivalent antifreeze mixture may be used, depending on operating temperatures. Open loops may also be used subject to the permits being obtained from the Environment Agency. Heat may be supplied to the dwelling either by a water-based heating system (water-to-water heat pump) or by an air distribution system (water-to-air heat pump).		
Air source heat pump (ASHP) systems	Air-to-water	Air-to-air
Air source heat pumps extract heat directly from the ambient air. Heat is supplied to the dwelling either by a water-based heating system (air-to-water heat pump) or by an air distribution system (air-to-air heat pump). Air source heat pumps may be single package or split systems.		
Supplementary information		
All heat pump systems are at their most efficient when the source temperature is as high as possible, the heat distribution temperature is as low as possible and pressure losses in air and water systems are kept to a minimum. If installed in a new dwelling, heat pumps should use refrigerants complying with the provisions of EC Regulation No 2037/2000. Heat pumps should be CE marked in accordance with applicable EU directives: e.g. the machinery safety, low voltage, pressure equipment and electromagnetic compatibility directives. If summer cooling is provided by the heat pump, it is recommended that condensate drainage from the indoor units is provided.		

9.2 Key terms

Coefficient of performance (COP) is a measure of the efficiency of a heat pump at specified source and sink temperatures, but may not accurately represent installed performance:

Heating COP = heat output / power input

% COP (COP × 100) is the heat generator efficiency.

COP is measured in accordance with the procedures in BS EN 14511:2013, *Air conditioners, liquid chilling packages and heat pumps with electrically driven compressors for space heating and cooling.*

Seasonal coefficient of performance (SCOP) is the overall coefficient of performance of the heat pump over the designated heating season. It makes general assumptions about the amount of auxiliary heating needed to top up the space and water heating available from the heat pump.

SCOP is measured in accordance with the procedures in BS EN 14825:2013, *Air conditioners, liquid chilling packages and heat pumps with electrically driven compressors for space heating and cooling. Testing and rating at part load conditions and calculation of seasonal performance.*

The National Calculation Methodology for calculating carbon dioxide emission rates from buildings uses SCOP.

Seasonal performance factor (SPF) is another measure of the operating performance of an electric heat pump over the season. It is the ratio of the heat delivered to the total electrical energy supplied over the season, but there are up to seven different ways to draw the system boundaries. For example, SPF_{H2} (which is SCOP) excludes auxiliary resistance heating whereas SPF_{H4} includes it – making a large difference.

SAP 2012 calculations use SPF – either measured values for products listed in the Product Characteristics Database, or the default values in Table 4a for products not listed there.

The Microgeneration Certification Scheme installation standard, MIS 3005, uses SPF to calculate system performance (although the heat pump product standard, MCS 007, currently specifies a minimum COP).

Seasonal primary energy efficiency ratio (SPEER) is an emerging rating figure reflecting the use of primary energy for all types of heat pump, fossil fuel boiler and gas-driven cogeneration technologies, as well as hybrid systems where solar heating or a heat pump is backed up with electric heating or a fossil fuel boiler.

Energy labelling with the SPEER will be mandatory from 2015 under the Energy Labelling Directive. Testing and rating will be in accordance with BS EN 14825, as for SCOP.

9.3 Warm water and hot water heat pumps

At the time of preparation of this guide, European Commission Regulation No 206/2012 sets standards for the SCOP of electrically-driven air-to-air heat pumps with an output ≤ 12 kW. There are currently no European test standards for part-load testing of air-to-air heat pumps with an output > 12 kW or for other types of heat pump, and the performance of these must be specified using COP obtained at the heating system rating conditions.

The current recommendations in this guide are that electrically-driven heat pumps should:

a. if air-to-air with an output ≤ 12 kW, have at least a SCOP 'D' rating for the median temperature range in BS EN 14825

b. or else have a COP which is not less than:

   i. 2.5 for space heating in new dwellings

   ii. 2.2 for space heating in existing dwellings

   iii. 2.0 for heating domestic hot water

c. meet the minimum standards for supply temperature, wet system radiator efficiency, installation and commissioning, hot water and controls in Table 36 for warm water and hot water heat pumps

d. meet the minimum standards for installation and controls in Table 37 for warm air heat pumps.

Table 36 Recommended minimum standards for warm water and hot water heat pumps (ground-to-water, water-to-water and air-to-water systems)

	Minimum standard	Supplementary information
1.0 Supply water temperatures and efficiency	**Underfloor heating** a. Supply water temperatures to the underfloor heating system should be in the range 30°C to 40°C for new buildings and 30°C to 55°C for existing systems.	See Section 7 of this guide on underfloor heating.
	Radiators b. High-efficiency radiators with high water volume should be utilised. c. Supply water temperature to the radiators should be in the range 40°C to 55°C.	Space heating may be sized to meet all or part of the space heating load. Secondary heating will be required if the heat pump is sized to meet part of the space heating load.
	Fan coil units d. Supply water temperature to the fan coil units should be in the range 35°C to 45°C.	Fan coil units may be utilised for heating only or for winter heating and summer cooling.

Table 36 Recommended minimum standards for warm water and hot water heat pumps (ground-to-water, water-to-water and air-to-water systems) *(continued)*

	Minimum standard	Supplementary information
2.0 Installation and commission- ing	a. The water distribution system should be arranged for reverse return operation or arranged with a low loss manifold system to maximise efficiency and ease commissioning and future maintenance. b. Pipework not contributing to the space heating should be insulated to prevent heat loss, following the guidance in the TIMSA guide. c. If summer cooling is provided by the heat pump, all water distribution pipework should be insulated to prevent condensation, following the guidance in the TIMSA guide. d. External pipework between the dwelling and the ground heat exchanger should be insulated, following the TIMSA guidance. e. The ground loop water circuit should be protected with an antifreeze solution and inhibitor as recommended by the heat pump manufacturer. f. Ground loops should be cleaned with a cleaning fluid and biocide as part of the commissioning process. g. The internal water distribution circuit should contain an inhibitor and may be protected by an antifreeze solution as recommended by the heat pump manufacturer. h. Ground loops should be filled with a heat transfer fluid. Installers should also refer to the equipment manufacturer's installation instructions for appropriate treatment products and special requirements for individual appliance models.	**Design** A pressurised water distribution system with expansion vessel is recommended. Constant water flow should be maintained through the heat pump. Pipe sizes should be in accordance with the manufacturer's recommendations. **Installation** Installation should be carried out by an installer approved by the manufacturer. If during installation access to the refrigeration circuit is needed, a competent refrigeration and air conditioning engineer holding a refrigerant handling certificate and an Engineering Services Skillcard should carry out the work. Exposed refrigeration pipework should be insulated and enclosed in protective trunking to limit accidental damage. Installation of the dwelling's water distribution system should be undertaken by a competent central heating specialist. **Guidance and standards** TIMSA *HVAC guidance for achieving compliance with Part L of the Building Regulations.* BS EN 378:2008 *Refrigerating systems and heat pumps. Safety and environmental requirements.* TR30 *Guide to good practice – heat pumps*, HVCA, July 2007. MIS 3005 *Requirements for contractors undertaking the supply, design, installation, set to work, commissioning and handover of microgeneration heat pump systems*, DECC.

Table 36 Recommended minimum standards for warm water and hot water heat pumps (ground-to-water, water-to-water and air-to-water systems) *(continued)*

	Minimum standard	Supplementary information
3.0 Domestic hot water (DHW)	a. For full heating, the heat pump and any supplementary domestic hot water heating should be capable of supplying water in the range 60°C to 65°C. This is applicable to ground-to-water, water-to-water and air-to-water type heat pumps. b. If the heat pump is not capable of supplying water at these temperatures, supplementary heating should be provided and controlled as described in other sections of this guide. Controls should include an auxiliary heating regime to 60°C or more for disinfection purposes. c. The domestic hot water system should have temperature control (e.g. a tank thermostat) and time control to optimise the time taken to heat the water.	The heat pump may be utilised for all or part of the DHW load. During the DHW heating period the heat pump may not necessarily be providing heated water to the space heating system.

4.0 Controls	a. Heat pump unit controls should include:
	
	  i. control of water pump operation (internal and external as appropriate)
	
	  ii. control of water temperature for the distribution system
	
	  iii. control of outdoor fan operation for air-to-water units
	
	  iv. defrost control of external airside heat exchanger for air-to-water systems
	
	  v. protection for water flow failure
	
	  vi. protection for high water temperature
	
	  vii. protection for high refrigerant pressure
	
	  viii. protection for air flow failure on air-to-water units.
	
	b. External controls should include:
	
	  i. weather compensation or internal temperature control
	
	  ii. timer or programmer for space heating.
	
	c. Minimum heat pump flow rates or volume requirements should be met. If all zones are thermostatically controlled, then a buffer would be an acceptable method of compliance.	

Table 37 Recommended minimum standards for warm air heat pumps (ground-to-air, water-to-air and air-to-air systems)

	Minimum standard	Supplementary information
1.0 Installation	a. Minimum clearances adjacent to all airflow paths, as recommended by the manufacturer, should be maintained. b. Pipe sizes should be in accordance with the manufacturer's recommendations. c. The refrigerant pipework on split systems should be insulated in line with the manufacturer's recommendations. d. If summer cooling is provided by the heat pump, provision should be made for condensate drainage from the indoor terminal units. e. For ground-to-air and water-to-air systems all external pipework between the dwelling and the external heat exchanger should be insulated following TIMSA guidance. f. For ground-to-air and water-to-air systems constant water flow should be maintained through the heat pump.	Installation should be carried out by an installer approved by the manufacturer. Installation that requires access to the refrigeration circuit, or the connection of split systems, should be carried out by a competent refrigeration and air conditioning engineer holding a refrigerant handling certificate and an Engineering Services Skillcard. TIMSA *HVAC guidance for achieving compliance with Part L of the Building Regulations*.

2.0 Controls	a. Heat pump unit controls should include:
	
	  i. control of room air temperature (if not provided externally)
	
	  ii. control of outdoor fan operation for air-to-air units
	
	  iii. defrost control of external airside heat exchanger for air-to-air systems
	
	  iv. control for secondary heating (if fitted) on air-to-air systems
	
	  v. control of external water pump operation for ground-to-air and water-to-air systems
	
	  vi. protection for high refrigerant pressure
	
	  vii. protection for indoor air flow failure
	
	  viii. protection for external air flow failure on air-to-air units
	
	  ix. protection for water flow failure on ground-to-air and water-to-air systems.
	
	b. External controls should include:
	
	  i. weather compensation or internal temperature control
	
	  ii. timer or programmer for space heating.
	
	c. Minimum heat pump flow rates or volume requirements should be met. If all zones are thermostatically controlled, then a buffer would be an acceptable method of compliance.	

Supplementary information

Guidance

Microgeneration Certification Scheme standard MIS 3005 *Requirements for contractors undertaking the supply, design, installation, set to work, commissioning and handover of microgeneration heat pump systems.*

Microgeneration Certification Scheme standard MIS 3007 *Product certification scheme requirements – heat pumps.*

Heat emitter guide for domestic heat pumps.
Available from http://www.microgenerationcertification.org/mcs-standards/installer-standards.

Design of low-temperature domestic heating systems – A guide for system designers and installers. FB59, IHS BRE Press. Available from www.brebookshop.com.

CE 82 Energy Efficiency Best Practice in Housing: *Domestic ground source heat pumps: design and installation of closed-loop systems.*

Heat Pump Association data sheet *Air-to-water heat pumps.*

HVCA TR30 *Guide to good practice: Heat pumps.*

Standards

BS EN 15450:2007 *Heating systems in buildings. Design of heat pump heating systems.*

BS EN 15316-4-2:2008 *Heating systems in buildings. Methods for calculation of system energy requirements and system efficiencies. Space heating generation systems, heat pump systems.*

BS EN 378-1:2008+A2:2012 *Refrigerating systems and heat pumps. Safety and environmental requirements. Basic requirements, definitions, classification and selection criteria.*

BS EN 378-2:2008+A2:2012 *Refrigerating systems and heat pumps. Safety and environmental requirements. Design, construction, testing, marking and documentation.*

BS EN 378-3:2008+A1:2012 *Refrigerating systems and heat pumps. Safety and environmental requirements. Installation site and personal protection.*

BS EN 378-4:2008+A1:2012 *Refrigerating systems and heat pumps. Safety and environmental requirements. Operation, maintenance, repair and recovery.*

ISO 13256-1:1998 *Water-source heat pumps. Testing and rating for performance. Water-to-air and brine-to-air heat pumps.*

ISO 13256-2:1998 *Water-source heat pumps. Testing and rating for performance. Water-to-water and brine-to-water heat pumps.*

Section 10: Comfort cooling

10.1 Scope of guidance

This section provides guidance on the specification of fixed mechanical comfort cooling systems and fans in dwellings to meet relevant energy efficiency requirements in the Building Regulations.

(Dwellings should always be designed to avoid or minimise the need for cooling through the appropriate use of solar control, secure ventilation and thermal mass.)

10.2 Air-cooled and water-cooled air conditioners

Cooling systems in new and existing dwellings should:

a. meet the minimum standards for efficiency in Table 38

b. be controlled to prevent simultaneous heating and cooling of the same space within the dwelling

c. comply with European Commission Regulation No 327/2011 for fans driven by motors with an electric input power between 125 W and 500 kW, and Regulation No 206/2012 for systems with a cooling capacity of up to 12 kW, both implementing Directive 2009/125/EC with regard to ecodesign requirements for energy-related products.

Table 38 Recommended minimum standards for air conditioner efficiency

Minimum standard	Supplementary information
a. Air-cooled air conditioners working in cooling mode should have an EER greater than 2.4.	Installation should be carried out by an installer approved by the manufacturer or supplier. The installer should be a competent refrigeration and air conditioning engineer with a valid refrigerant handling certificate.
b. Water-cooled air conditioners working in cooling mode should have an EER greater than 2.5.	
c. Fixed air conditioners should have an energy efficiency classification equal to or better than Class C in Schedule 3 of the labelling scheme adopted under The Energy Information (Household Air Conditioners) (No 2) Regulations, SI 2005/1726.	Exposed refrigeration pipework should be insulated and enclosed in protective trunking to limit accidental damage. See: www.eurovent-certification.com

British Standards

BS EN 14511-2:2013 *Air conditioners, liquid chilling packages and heat pumps with electrically driven compressors for space heating and cooling. Test conditions.*

BS EN 14511-4:2013 *Air conditioners, liquid chilling packages and heat pumps with electrically driven compressors for space heating and cooling. Requirements.*

Section 11: Solar water heating

11.1 Scope of guidance

This section provides guidance on the specification of solar water heating for dwellings to meet relevant energy efficiency requirements in the Building Regulations.

The guidance in this section covers indirect solar systems with a collector area of less than 20 m² and solar heated water storage of less than 440 litres. It does not cover 'direct' solar systems[18] or systems intended to contribute exclusively to space heating or systems providing heat exclusively to heat swimming pools. It should be used in conjunction with the guidance on water heating contained in the fuel-based sections of this guide.

11.2 Indirect systems

Indirect solar heating systems installed as new systems and replacement systems should meet the minimum standards for:

a. collector certification, identification and testing, collector primary loop transfer fluid, circulation pump power, heat-exchanger sizing, system control, solar pre-heated water storage and system preparation in Table 39

b. system labelling and commissioning in Table 40

c. insulating pipes in a solar primary system in Table 41.

Supplementary information

When work is carried out on an existing indirect solar hot water system, it is recommended that the system controls and insulation should be upgraded in line with the standards for new systems.

Table 39 Recommended minimum standards for indirect solar water heating

	Minimum standard	Supplementary information
1.0 **Allowance for collector shading**	a. No minimum provision.	Solar collectors should be sited in unshaded locations wherever possible. Where this is unachievable or in cases of significant or heavy shading or significant variance to the optimum orientation and tilt (i.e. normal pitch roofs facing between SE and SW), then an allowance for the loss of performance should be made when sizing the collector area according to the factors indicated in SAP 2012 Appendix H.

---

18   The Microgeneration Certification Scheme Standard MIS 3001 includes guidance on solar heating systems with a dedicated solar volume that is below the minimum recommended for indirect systems. SAP 2012 Appendix H sets out rules for estimating the annual energy performance of solar heating systems, including direct systems.

Table 39 Recommended minimum standards for indirect solar water heating *(continued)*

	Minimum standard	Supplementary information
2.0 Solar collector certification	a. Collectors should be independently certified to comply with all required tests for safety and thermal performance, and for reporting and identification according to BS EN 12975-1:2006+A1:2010 *Thermal solar systems and components. Solar collectors. General requirements.*	Copies of the full test report should be made available upon request.
3.0 Primary circuit fluid	a. The transfer fluid in the collector primary loop should be chosen so as not to deposit limescale, sludge, ice or other solids that could either restrict circulation or impair the rate of heat transfer within the absorber.	In secondary systems, measures to reduce the formation of limescale should be considered so that performance is not significantly affected.
4.0 Circulation pump power	a. The electrical input power of the primary pump in the solar system should be less than 50 W or 2% of peak thermal power of collector, whichever is the higher.	
5.0 Heat-exchanger sizing	a. The heat exchanger between a solar primary and secondary system should be sized so that not less than 0.1 m^2 or equivalent of heat exchanger area is provided per 1 m^2 of solar collector net absorber area.	A heat exchanger reduces the possibility of clogging and deposition due to dirt, scale or similar impurities that could reduce the system performance. Heat exchangers and store connections should be sized and located to promote a low return temperature to the solar collector. Solar heat exchangers are often sized larger than those usually used on gas- or oil-based primary systems owing to the lower temperature of transfer.
6.0 System control	a. Solar domestic hot water (DHW) system controls should be fitted to: i. maximise the useful energy gain from the solar collectors into the system's dedicated storage ii. minimise the accidental loss of stored energy by the solar DHW system, whether originating from solar collectors, cold intake or auxiliary heat sources iii. ensure that hot water produced by back-up (auxiliary) heat sources is not used when adequate grade solar pre-heated water is available iv. provide a means of control consistent with the solar system being hydraulically (inherently) secure against the adverse effects of excessive primary temperatures and pressures v. where a separate DHW heating appliance is pre-heated by a solar system, control the appliance where possible such that no extra heat is added if the target temperature is already satisfied from the pre-heat vessel vi. inform the end user of the system's correct function and performance at all times.	

Table 39 Recommended minimum standards for indirect solar water heating *(continued)*

	Minimum standard	Supplementary information
7.0 **Solar pre-heated water storage**	a. Vented copper hot water storage vessels should comply with the heat loss and back-up heating heat exchanger requirements of BS 1566-1:2002 *Copper indirect cylinders for domestic purposes. Open vented copper cylinders. Requirements and test methods.* b. Unvented hot water storage system products should comply with BS EN 12897:2006 or an equivalent standard. c. Primary storage systems should meet the insulation requirements of sections 4.3.1 or 4.3.2 of the Hot Water Association *Performance specification for thermal stores.*	Vented copper hot water cylinders should carry clear labelling on the product such as a BSI Kitemark, registered firm status or reference to an equivalent quality control scheme. Vented cylinders which are not of copper construction should be labelled as complying with the heat loss and heat exchanger requirements of BS 1566-1:2002. Due to the higher than normal storage temperatures in primary stores, it is very important that they are well insulated.

8.0
Volume of solar pre-heated water
	a. The ratio of solar heated water storage volume to collector area should be as follows:
	
	  i. The dedicated solar storage volume, V_s, should be at least 25 litres (or equivalent heat capacity) per net square metre of the solar collector absorber area.
	
	  ii. Alternatively, V_s should be a volume (or equivalent heat capacity) which is equivalent to at least 80% of the daily hot water demand, V_d (as defined by SAP 2012).
		Collector area is measured as effective aperture or net absorber area, whichever is smaller.
		
		A separate pre-heat storage vessel should be considered wherever possible.

Table 39 Recommended minimum standards for indirect solar water heating *(continued)*

	Minimum standard	Supplementary information
9.0 System preparation and water treatment	**New build**	Parts of BS 7593:2006 *Code of practice for treatment of water in domestic hot water central heating systems* may assist in flushing and cleaning procedures. *Legionnaire's disease: The control of legionella bacteria in water systems.* Approved code of practice and guidance, HSE Books.

New build

a. Solar primary circuits should be thoroughly cleaned with an appropriate cleaner and flushed through with solar heat transfer fluid before filling with the solar heat transfer fluid.

b. Systems should be filled with a heat transfer fluid containing a volatile inhibitor package, capable of protecting the system from frost and corrosion at all operating temperatures.

c. Installers should refer to the equipment manufacturer's installation instructions for appropriate treatment products and special requirements for individual appliance models.

d. Where mains water is used to fill the solar primary circuit and the total water hardness exceeds 200 parts per million, provision should be made to reduce the limescale.

Existing installations

e. Solar thermal systems should be cleaned with an appropriate cleaner formulated to remove build-up of degradation films from exhausted heat transfer fluids, then flushed through with fresh solar heat transfer fluid.

f. Systems should be filled with a heat transfer fluid containing a volatile inhibitor package, capable of protecting the system from frost and corrosion at all operating temperatures.

g. Installers should refer to the equipment manufacturer's installation instructions for appropriate treatment products and special requirements for individual appliance models.

Table 40 Recommended minimum standards for labelling, commissioning and documentation for solar hot water systems

	Minimum standard	Supplementary information
1.0 Labelling of solar collectors and hot water stores	a. All solar collectors should have a visible and durable label displaying all information required according to BS EN 12975-1:2006+A1:2010, and including at least the following: i. name of manufacturer ii. collector type iii. serial number iv. year of production v. gross area of collector vi. aperture area of collector vii. net absorber area of collector viii. maximum operation pressure ix. stagnation temperature at 1000 W/m^2 and 30°C ambient x. volume of heat transfer fluid xi. weight of empty solar collector. b. All hot water storage vessels should carry a label with the following information: i. name of manufacturer ii. nominal overall capacity in litres iii. dedicated solar capacity in litres iv. standing heat loss in kWh/day v. type of vessel vi. back-up heating heat exchanger performance in kW (where present) vii. solar heating heat exchanger performance in kW.	In addition to the minimum provision for labelling of hot water storage vessels, labelling with the following information is also recommended: • Total net fluid content of secondary volume normally heated by each heat exchanger, where present ($\pm$ 1.0 litre). • The type, fluid content, maximum pressure and surface area of all heat exchangers.
2.0 Commissioning	a. A signed and dated commissioning certificate should be completed to confirm the equipment has been correctly installed and to record key safety and operational features. b. As a minimum, the commissioning certificate should record the following details of the solar system: i. net or aperture area of solar collector ii. minimum ambient temperature without freeze damage to components iii. location of device and method for controlling over-pressure iv. location of the electrical isolating switch v. type of circulation fluid vi. circulation rate of collector circuit vii. location of device for protecting against overheating of solar heated water.	A signed commissioning certificate, certifying that the equipment is safe, legal and fit for its intended purpose, should be handed over to the dwelling owner or user as applicable. A separate certificate is required to cover the installation and commissioning of the hot water storage vessels and appliances within a solar DHW system. A commissioning engineer should be a competent person who can personally testify by signature and date that the equipment has been commissioned.

Table 40 Recommended minimum standards for labelling, commissioning and documentation for solar hot water systems *(continued)*

	Minimum standard	Supplementary information
3.0 Document-ation		Information provided to the dwelling owner or user should include: • user manual • warranty information • a recommended maintenance schedule • commissioning certificate • full contact details of the installer.

Table 41 Recommended minimum standards for insulation of pipework in solar hot water systems

Minimum standard	Supplementary information
a. All pipes of a solar primary system should be insulated throughout the length of the circuit. b. All other pipes connected to hot water storage vessels, including the vent pipe, should be insulated for at least 1 metre from their points of connection to the cylinder, or insulated up to the point where they become concealed. c. Pipes should be insulated with appropriately labelled materials and in line with the TIMSA guide. d. Heat loss values should not exceed the values in the Supplementary information column.	The insulation should be suitably rated for the maximum foreseeable pipe temperature applicable, and where external also be resistant to vermin attack and climatic degradation. In a dwelling that already has a solar hot water system, it is recommended that the insulation should be upgraded in line with these minimum provisions where significant work, such as change of solar storage, is carried out. A fully-filled or drainback solar hot water system can have a pipe service temperature of 150°C. The insulation material should be specified to accommodate this temperature. An EPDM based rubber would normally be a minimum requirement for such an application. Any insulation specified should be better than 0.044 W/(m·K) at 40°C mean and the insulation diameter should be 87% of the pipe diameter.

Pipe outside diameter (mm)	Maximum heat loss (W/m)
8	7.06
10	7.23
12	7.35
15	7.89
22	9.12
28	10.07
35	11.08
42	12.19
54	14.12

In assessing the thickness of insulation required, standardised conditions should be assumed in all compliance calculations, based on a horizontal pipe at 40°C in still air at 15°C.

Further guidance on converting heat loss limits to thicknesses of insulation for specific thermal conductivities is available in the TIMSA *HVAC guidance for achieving compliance with Part L of the Building Regulations*.

Insulation for pipework in unheated areas

It may be necessary to protect water-carrying pipework in unheated areas against freezing. Further guidance is available in:

- BS 5422:2009 *Method for specifying thermal insulating materials for pipes, tanks, vessels, ductwork and equipment operating within the temperature range of -40°C to +700°C.*

- BRE Report No 262 *Thermal insulation: avoiding risks*, 2002 edition.

Further information

Microgeneration Certification Scheme standard MIS 3001 *Requirements for contractors undertaking the supply, design, installation, set to work, commissioning and handover of solar heating microgeneration systems.*

Energy Efficiency Best Practice in Housing CE131 *Solar water heating systems. Guidance for professionals, conventional indirect models.*

CIBSE *Solar heating design and installation guide.*

CE51/GIL59 *Central Heating System Specifications (CHeSS)*, 2005.

Section 12: Lighting

12.1 Scope of guidance

This section provides guidance on the specification of fixed internal and external lighting for new and existing dwellings to meet relevant energy efficiency requirements in the Building Regulations.

12.2 Key terms

Circuit-watt means the power consumed in lighting circuits by lamps and, where applicable, their associated control gear (including transformers and drivers) and power factor correction equipment.

Light fitting means a fixed light or lighting unit that can comprise one or more lamps and lampholders, control gear and an appropriate housing. The control gear may be integrated in the lamp or located elsewhere in or near to the fixed light.

Fixed external lighting means lighting fixed to an external surface of the dwelling supplied from the occupier's electrical system. It excludes lighting in common areas of blocks of flats and in other communal accessways.

12.3 Internal and external lighting

Fixed internal and external lighting should meet the minimum standards for efficacy and controls in Table 42.

Table 42 Recommended minimum standards for fixed internal and external lighting

	Minimum standard	Supplementary information
Fixed internal lighting	a. In the areas affected by the building work, provide low energy light fittings (fixed lights or lighting units) that number not less than three per four of all the light fittings in the main dwelling spaces of those areas (excluding infrequently accessed spaces used for storage, such as cupboards and wardrobes).	Light fittings may be either: • dedicated fittings which will have separate control gear and will take only low energy lamps (e.g. pin based fluorescent or compact fluorescent lamps), or • standard fittings supplied with low energy lamps with integrated control gear (e.g. bayonet or Edison screw base compact fluorescent lamps).
	b. Low energy light fittings should have lamps with a luminous efficacy greater than 45 lamp lumens per circuit-watt and a total output greater than 400 lamp lumens.	Light fittings with GLS tungsten filament lamps or tungsten halogen lamps would not meet the standard.
	c. Light fittings whose supplied power is less than 5 circuit-watts are excluded from the overall count of the total number of light fittings.	The Energy Saving Trust publication GIL20 *Low energy domestic lighting* gives guidance on identifying suitable locations for fixed energy efficient lighting. A single switch should normally operate no more than six light fittings with a maximum total load of 100 circuit-watts.

Fixed external lighting	Where fixed external lighting is installed, provide light fittings with the following characteristics:
	
	a. Either:
	
	  i. lamp capacity not greater than 100 lamp-watts per light fitting, and
	
	  ii. all lamps automatically controlled so as to switch off after the area lit by the fitting becomes unoccupied, and
	
	  iii. all lamps automatically controlled so as to switch off when daylight is sufficient.
	
	b. Or:
	
	  i. lamp efficacy greater than 45 lumens per circuit-watt, and
	
	  ii. all lamps automatically controlled so as to switch off when daylight is sufficient, and
	
	  iii. light fittings controllable manually by occupants.	

Supplementary information

British Standards

BS EN 15193:2007 *Energy performance of buildings. Energy requirements for lighting.*

Other related documents

CE80 *Domestic lighting innovations*, Energy Efficiency Best Practice in Housing.

CE61 *Energy efficient lighting – guidance for installers and specifiers*, Energy Saving Trust.

EP84 *Housing for people with sight loss*, Thomas Pocklington Trust Design Guide.

IP412 *Making the most of your sight: Improve the lighting in your home*, RNIB and Thomas Pocklington Trust.

Energy Saving Trust best practice standards

The Energy Saving Trust sets best practice 'Energy Saving Recommended' (ESR) standards for lamps that cover not only energy efficiency, but also other aspects of quality including colour rendering, warm-up time, product life and power factor. It is advisable to install only ESR low energy lamps in dwellings.

Section 13: Micro-combined heat and power

13.1 Scope of guidance

This section provides guidance on the specification of micro-combined heat and power (micro-CHP) packages for dwellings to meet relevant energy efficiency requirements in the Building Regulations.

The guidance covers micro-CHP systems with an electrical output less than 5 kWe which are:

- heat-led

- capable of exporting electricity to the grid, and

- controlled in such a way as to avoid heat dumping.

13.2 Key terms

Heating plant emission rate (HPER) is the annual carbon dioxide emissions from fuel and power consumed by the heating plant, offset by the emissions saved as a result of any electricity generated by the heating plant, divided by the heat output over a year. It is measured in units of kg of carbon dioxide per kWh. To calculate HPER it is necessary to know the plant size ratio. Note: The HPER includes any auxiliary space and water heating that may be necessary, i.e. it represents the performance of all heating plant needed to provide space and water heating service to the building, assuming a standard demand pattern.

Plant size ratio (PSR) is defined as the nominal heat output of the heating plant divided by the design heat loss (the average heat loss of the building on a cold day with a temperature differential of 24.2°C). Note: For a given heat demand, the PSR determines the part-load condition for the heating plant.

13.3 Micro-CHP systems

a. For new systems, the HPER of the micro-CHP package (calculated as in sub-paragraph c. below) should be no greater than the carbon dioxide emission factor for the fuel divided by the minimum efficiency for a regular boiler using that fuel, at the PSR determined as in sub-paragraph b. below. The design heat loss of the dwelling should be calculated using the Energy Saving Trust's *Whole house boiler sizing method for houses and flats*[19].

b. The PSR for the micro-CHP system when operating in the intended dwelling should be calculated as defined in paragraph 13.2 above.

c. The HPER of the micro-CHP system should be calculated at the PSR determined in sub-paragraph b. above, using the methodology set out in DECC's Annual Performance Method (APM)[20] and the performance data for the micro-CHP package established by testing according to BSI PAS 67[21].

---

19 Energy Saving Trust CE54 *Whole house boiler sizing method for houses and flats*. This is an interactive calculator available from the Energy Saving Trust at www.energysavingtrust.org.uk/housingbuildings/publications. The design heat loss in kW is the basic design heat loss in box U (from the 2010 edition).

20 *Method to evaluate the annual energy performance of micro-cogeneration heating systems in dwellings* (APM), SAP 2012 revision, DECC. Available from www.bre.co.uk/sap2012.

21 BSI PAS 67:2008 *Laboratory tests to determine the heating and electrical performance of heat-led micro-cogeneration packages primarily intended for heating dwellings.*

Supplementary information

British Standards

BS EN 15316-4-4:2007 *Heating systems in buildings. Method for calculation of system energy requirements and system efficiencies. Heat generation systems, building-integrated cogeneration systems.*

Other documents

Appendix N of SAP 2012 *Method to evaluate the annual energy performance of micro-cogeneration heating systems in dwellings.*

BSRIA BG 2/2007 *CHP for existing buildings: Guidance on design and installation.*

Microgeneration Certification Scheme standard, MIS 3007-2 *Requirements for contractors undertaking the design, supply, installation, set to work, commissioning and handover of a domestic hot water system containing an electricity-led micro-cogeneration package.*

Connecting a microgeneration system to a domestic or similar electrical installation (in parallel with the mains supply), Best Practice Guide, the Electrical Safety Council.

Section 14: Heating system circulators

14.1 Scope of guidance

This section provides guidance on the specification of heating system glandless circulators, both standalone and integrated in products, to meet relevant energy efficiency requirements in the Building Regulations.

14.2 Circulators

Heating system glandless circulators up to 2.5 kW, provided with new systems or as replacements in existing systems in dwellings, should meet the minimum standards for energy efficiency in Table 43.

Table 43 Recommended minimum standards for heating system glandless circulators	
Minimum standard	**Supplementary information**
In accordance with European Commission Regulation No 622/2012 (amending 641/2009) implementing Directive 2005/32/EC with regard to ecodesign requirements for glandless circulators up to 2.5 kW: a. From 1 January 2013, standalone glandless circulators, other than those specifically designed for primary circuits of thermal solar systems and of heat pumps, should have an Energy Efficiency Index (EEI) no greater than 0.27. b. From 1 August 2015, standalone glandless circulators and glandless circulators integrated in products should have an Energy Efficiency Index (EEI) no greater than 0.23.	Further information and guidance, including a list of approved glandless domestic circulators, is available at www.bpma.org.uk.

Appendix A: Abbreviations

APM	Annual Performance Method
ASHP	Air source heat pump
BS	British Standard
BSI	British Standards Institute
CHeSS	Central Heating System Specifications
CHP	Combined heat and power
CO_2	Carbon dioxide
COP	Coefficient of performance
DCLG	Department for Communities and Local Government
DECC	Department of Energy and Climate Change
DHW	Domestic hot water
EEI	Energy Efficiency Index
EER	Energy efficiency ratio
EN	European Norm (standard)
ESR	Energy Saving Recommended
GSHP	Ground source heat pump
HPER	Heating plant emission rate
HVAC	Heating, ventilation and air conditioning
LPG	Liquified petroleum gas
PAS	Publicly Available Specification
PCDB	Product Characteristics Database
PSR	Plant size ratio
RHI	Renewable Heat Incentive
SAP	Standard Assessment Procedure
SCOP	Seasonal coefficient of performance
SEDBUK	Seasonal Efficiency of Domestic Boilers in the UK
SEER	Seasonal energy efficiency ratio
SFP	Specific fan power
SI	Statutory Instrument
SPEER	Seasonal primary energy efficiency ratio
SPF	Seasonal performance factor
TER	Target carbon dioxide emission rate
TRV	Thermostatic radiator valve
WSHP	Water source heat pump